Praise for *Let Your G*

D0379191

"*Let Your Goddess Grow!* will jump-start your spiritual journey if you haven't already begun. It illustrates why it is possible to manifest an abundant life with a proper mind and heart set. Read it and feel empowered!"

Arielle Ford, author of Hot Chocolate for the Mystical Soul

"Imagine a powerful woman who awakens to the truth about herself. A courageous woman who assumes her rightful place in the human community. A wise woman whose beliefs are reflected in her self-understanding, relationships, and livelihood. Charlene Proctor invites us to imagine this woman into being, for the sake of the planet."

Patricia Lynn Reilly, author of Imagine a Woman
and A God Who Looks Like Me

"Charlene Proctor is a savvy, modern-day priestess who brings the ancient wisdom of the Goddess into everyday life. Her step-by-step approach to evoking the power of the divine feminine is empowering and inspiring. If you are ready to get in touch with the Goddess in you, then this book is like manna from heaven."

Rev. Laurie Sue Brockway, author of A Goddess Is a Girl's
Best Friend: A Divine Guide to Find Love, Success and
Happiness and Wedding Goddess: A Divine Guide to
Transforming Wedding Stress into Wedding Bliss

"A balanced life embraces both the masculine and feminine energies of the soul. Charlene Proctor shows us how to do this brilliantly – this is essential reading for all men and women who seek deep meaning and fulfillment in their lives."

Lance Secretan, PhD, author of Inspire! What
Great Leaders Do and The Way of the Tiger

LET YOUR GODDESS GROW!

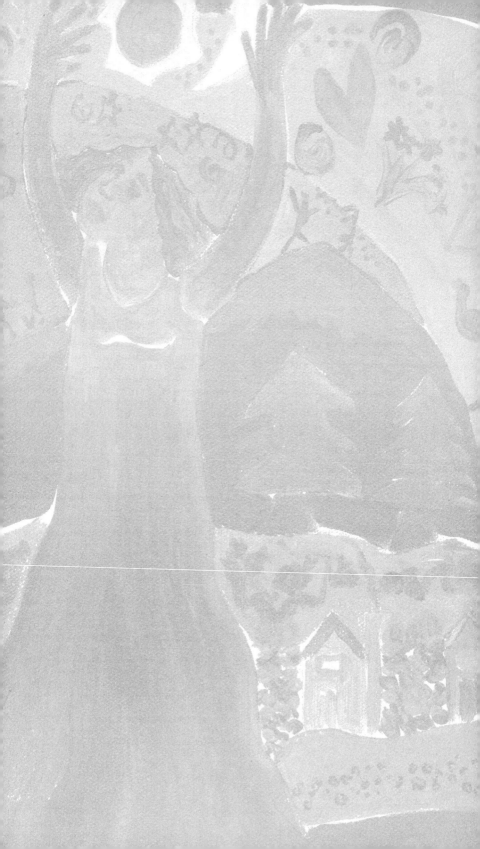

LET YOUR GODDESS GROW!

7 Spiritual Lessons on female Power and Positive Thinking

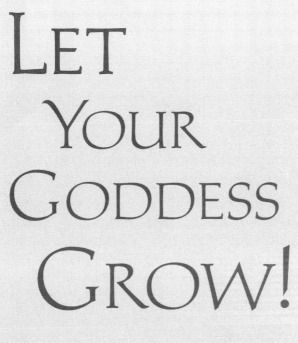

CHARLENE M. PROCTOR, PhD

*For all women in the universe
who desire to become who they truly are,
which is their divine self:
this book is for you.*

CONTENTS

Lesson Six

Corporate Soul: Use Spirit and Strength to
Guide Work Life   168

Lesson Seven

The Divine Feminine: Bring Mother God into Your Work and Life   204

Managing Life

*We're fragmented into all these little
parts and roles we have to play.*

– Julie, education administrator

Intuitively, I know I've lived many lifetimes, and none more interesting than the one I'm living now. However, being born an old soul
somehow did not excuse me from the same job I share with you –
and that is learning to craft a positive attitude about daily adversity. With a set of mental thought patterns to process our soul journey wisely and lovingly, we can become observers of our own lives.
If we hold this attitude firmly, our perceptions of people, career
paths, or even our living conditions change dramatically, allowing us to experience our environment in wonderful ways. We can
sift out what we want to include in the day's lesson and discard the
rest, feeling in control, no longer running on automatic programs.
We can feel victorious, energized by circumstances, not victimized.
All of a sudden, we notice we have created a fabulous reality based
upon our intentions.

A lot has been broadcast from the self-help community about
the importance of "stepping into a vision of who you are" as a prerequisite to having a good life. What does this mean? Our modern-
day mystics and philosophers are referring to self-understanding.
The self is your rendition of the spirit within you, your individual
spark of divinity. Your God/Goddess within is the true self that you
become over time. It constitutes your journey to being whole.

Realizing our own divinity, then using it to create a reality free
from angst and disappointment, is about living in conscious awareness of who we are, all the time. And we practice being divine by

making choices based in the present, using a creative license to choose what we want. If we recognize the Divine within and identify intimately with that idea, so there is no differentiation between what is God and what is us, then we are capable of anything. Our choices, just like the universe, become limitless. Our purpose, then, in this collective soul journey we share, is to become that which is within. It is to become our God-self. It is our inheritance, our innate gift and natural state.

I have not always been this smart. Like you, I have stumbled from one hard lesson to another over the course of many years, wondering why I seemed to revisit the same type of relationships or never felt in charge of my destiny. Why did the same patterns emerge in my career paths? The same disappointments? From bitterness over family matters to love gone astray, I found myself thinking "Life happens" or "It was never meant to be" far too often, as an unspoken acceptance of my lack of ability to overcome.

Beginning as children, we readily accept conditioning by such mantras of non-control, turning our power over to other ideas, food, relationships, religion, or materialism. By adulthood, we gather quite a large collection of anesthetics, choosing to bed down with them for long winters of discontent, blaming outside circumstances for our reality. Only we find we aren't any closer to our goals the following spring; we've just invested more energy convincing ourselves why it's not time to receive our good. And this is our biggest mistake. Life is not a nuisance to push through. It is designed to be so much more, and I think our shared experiences, living within the genius we call the universal creation, all lead to the same signpost, reading: *Thoughts Create Reality. This Way.* It is our choice whether to travel on that path of enlightenment or not.

The complexity that permeates our lives has little to do with what we have completed on the to-do list and much to do with our difficulty in experiencing the life we want. There is no plot against us. We've outlined these challenges for our own self-development because we are trying to leave ourselves clues that we are mentally capable of overcoming our environment. We are attempting to teach

SAVE
63%

BUSINESS REPLY MAIL

FIRST-CLASS MAIL   PERMIT NO. 22   TAMPA FL

POSTAGE WILL BE PAID BY ADDRESSEE

Health

PO BOX 62527
TAMPA FL 33662-5271

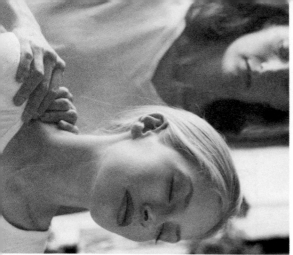

Give Yourself a Break

SAVE 63% off cover price

on **Health** magazine!

YES, I want HEALTH! Please start my one-year (10 issue) subscription to the magazine of great food, real beauty and total wellness. I'll pay only $12.97 and save 63% off the cover price.

NAME

ADDRESS

CITY   STATE   ZIP

EMAIL ADDRESS

www.health.com

Plus sales tax if applicable. Offer good in the U.S. only. Allow 4 weeks for delivery. *Health* is published 10 times a year. Cover price $3.99.

HAAD9B8

ourselves that we have the ability, present in our own minds, to experience the world as a creator, living life fully and consciously aware. We *can* see the results from our thinking. It only takes practice!

HOW WE BLOW IT

Rather than seeking within for power to create joyful lives, too often we look to the environment or relationships. Naturally, we crave reinforcement and praise. Who doesn't feel good when a sign arrives, encouraging us to keep putting one foot in front of the other? *Feeling* we make a difference is important, but we get into trouble when we function completely on automatic thought patterns to get the positive strokes.

Physiologically speaking, we wire our brains by using our associative memory – our associations with people, places, things, times, or events – and assigning emotions to those associations. Associative memory causes neurons in the brain to form a connection and when enough connect, a whole series will fire. That's called a neural network. Neural nets are developed by repetition. They help us function by providing our bodies with the ability to operate automatically when doing tasks such as brushing our teeth, walking, or typing. But because humans are complex beings, our bodies are highly integrated with our minds. Emotions associated with the complex skill sets required for ordinary tasks can become triggered automatically, affecting our behavior and our bodies by the production of chemicals. Our bodies begin to rely upon those chemicals. No kidding – scientists have found we can be addicted to our emotions!

Automatic programs don't serve us well when we rely upon them to propel us through life. For example, if you had abusive parents, you may have created memories of that relationship. Over years of repetition, you might have created an automatic program around this set of memories, which included certain emotions such as low self-esteem, anger, or resentment. Emotions begin to be problematic only to the degree that we are unconsciously surrendering to them in ways that don't serve our highest good. How can we recognize when this happens?

An example would be the automatic program that kicks in when something triggers your memories of your parents. You respond to people who remind you of your parents, or other authority figures, in the same way chemically. Most of the time, we don't even realize our dependency on these old programs that prevent us from experiencing healthy new relationships. Old programs affect our present-day circumstances, clouding our judgments and blocking opportunities for wonderful experiences because we are using old information, responses, and body chemistry to interpret the way things are today. It's not an accurate assessment of reality.

What can you learn from this quick tutorial in Brain 101? If you produce the same outcomes in your life, over and over again, you may be playing out what is, in fact, an old program in your head. You are recreating the same conditions to produce the same chemicals your body craves. For example, you may surround yourself with people who make you feel the way your parents made you feel, so that you have an anger outlet. Or you might substitute loneliness for love because you don't want to open yourself up to the possibility of rejection. Until the pattern of memory is broken by detaching from emotions you associate with a past relationship, you will continue to search unconsciously for similar experiences. Why? Our bodies naturally seek the chemical comfort. And many of us rely upon such automatic programs without even realizing it! We are more chemically attached to our bodies than we think, often making present-day choices based upon messages from bodies and minds that are seated in the past.

However, there is hope. Because our brains are more elastic than scientists originally thought, we can actually mold them by creating new programs that help us function. It doesn't take any technical expertise. We must simply be strong enough to *choose* what we want to experience, exercising free will. And we need to remember that the conscious mind is composed of power and intention. To produce change in our environment, *we need to consciously change*. It requires effort!

Fortunately, with the blending of quantum theory, neurophysiology, nanotechnology, brain imaging, mysticism, and some plain common sense, experts are finally confirming what we already intuitively know: we are in charge of creating our own reality. Their reasoning? If we continue to build a positive and loving mindset (a memory of our associations with people, places, things, events, and times) that helps us interact with the world in the *present moment*, life is *perceived* as a positive experience. We can *create* new memories to inform a new, present-day reality. Soon our bodies accept it, and we see external changes in our lives which become proof of our own efforts.

We can prune our old connections in our brains, dismantling old networks that no longer serve us well. We can create new neural nets just by practice. Just by opening to the concept of forgiveness, we can shatter defense mechanisms, release old perceptions of relationships, and consciously create room for the really good emotions. Reality is based upon how our brains are wired and a good attitude. *Everyone* has the same opportunity to rewire, and realizing this can either liberate us or hold us back. People are already exploring this opportunity with great success. It's called the conscious awareness movement.

Affirmations Help Reprogram Your Brain

It takes a lot of awareness to mentally and emotionally clean house. If we regularly experience self-doubt, unworthiness, or fear, we can arrest the thought process (by learning to control the stimulus that turns those emotions on) and gracefully move our minds to new ways of being, such as receptivity to self-love, opportunity, confidence, abundance, or adventure. We can observe our circumstances objectively and gain dominion over life, feeling emotions we want to experience and rejecting those we don't. Science now suggests we can measure the bodily effects of conscious awareness and positive thinking in the form of more energy, clearer thinking, stronger immune systems, and enhanced reasoning power.

This book, in the most practical, lighthearted way, points to where your stresses might be found. It gets you to think about how you might have created past patterns of negative thinking. To change your reality, you first need to construct new neural networks – new patterns of thinking. It's a discipline learned over time, but our bodies are designed to participate in this conscious process. How do we get started?

Training the mind is part of living in conscious awareness of our environment. It is helpful to recognize and name old, useless emotions: for example, feeling that your needs come last, fear, or low self-esteem. Then you can repeat positive statements, such as affirmations, with sincere belief and conscious intent. Affirmations are present-tense statements that assume that what you declare is real and present. The idea is not to mask negativity, but to consciously open the mind and body to life-affirming energy and thoughts. The more you practice, the greater will be the level of acceptance of each thought. An affirmation is simply a positive statement, a declaration to the universe that you choose to take the upper hand and that you never accept anything less than what you deserve. My affirmations are deeper and more complete self-help messages we can use to overhaul stale thoughts when the impulse hits. They are prayerfully contemplative, encouraging you to retain a spiritual focus on the big picture.

Let Your Goddess Grow! tutors you to recognize negative thinking before it becomes a habit. It includes seven lessons on becoming more attuned to the thoughts and emotions which give you the foundation of success at work and home. These lessons will help you refocus your energy and intentions. You'll learn how to thwart negativity by shifting your thought patterns throughout the day. Remember, you must *choose* to see something negative in a positive light and reprogram your response to that stress. When your reactions change, you can begin to cultivate a new life, filled with robustness, prosperity, love, good health, and happiness.

Three Positive Thinking Challenges for Women

We can't let go. Through my own real-world research, I have a few observations about the way women think. Over the years, I have interviewed many people, mostly women, and I've asked them all the same questions: What really slows you down? What interferes with your thought process and gets you spiraling down into a negative state? How do you rely upon your wisdom tradition to navigate through disappointment and chaos? And how would you change? Women agree that they need more discipline in shifting away from negative thought patterns and less energy spent on self-doubt. And they waste too much time analyzing the bad stuff.

Women are the supreme creatures of over-analysis. I can relate to this. We like to rehash an incident over and over until finally we are ready to let it go, which drives the men in our lives nuts. The problem is that once we release a negative experience, we just forget about it temporarily; instead, we should make peace with it. We don't view letting it go as an opportunity for transformation and refinement. If we arrested the impulse to over-analyze closer to when it entered our minds, we would save time and energy that we could spend on making positive change.

Part of the problem is a consequence of the pace of modern life, which forces us to operate on autopilot. We have simply lost the art of living in conscious awareness. Women are so busy managing their multiple lives that they believe they don't have time to take mental and emotional inventory of every negative occurrence. They feel compelled to provide balance in everyone's world but their own, juggling homes, children, careers, travel, and elderly parents, and they put far too much energy into struggling against aging. In their efforts to achieve unrealistic perfection, they give up the desire to override old programming and put self-observation at the bottom of the list. Women who spend years living by the expectations of others, unable to separate what they want from the intimate worlds they tend to, are devastated rather than liberated by middle age.

To weed out old programming and get on a positive thinking track, women need to develop the good habit of taking mental inventory *immediately* after they experience stress and strife, so that they can release them permanently. They need to take time to self-examine, rather than letting all the little things build up until they turn into one big thing, which usually happens at the worst possible moment, such as twenty minutes before the in-laws come to visit. They need to accept the greatest and most complete vision of who they are: an empowered and marvelous spark of the Divine.

It is possible to demonstrate exactly what we desire from our careers, relationships, and home life without compromising who we are in the process. Our world is and always will be a reflection of what is in our heads as long as we have the discipline to let go, devote more time to being rather than doing, and enjoy the ride.

We must override old cultural messages. Although women's lives have vastly improved in the last few centuries, doubt still exists in many women's minds that they are as powerful as men. I'll admit that it is difficult to break through the last remaining barriers in organizations, political structures, and even old-world family ideology. As women discover the power of their own thoughts in creating the world they want, they will inevitably have to discover something sacred about themselves. Women have a lot of old programming to overcome, perhaps more than men have, because of society's residual messages from old cultural values and religions.

If women want to discover their own thoughts and not live the thoughts of others, they must make a supreme effort to disconnect from what appears to be convention and be willing to risk rejection. There is no greater example of convention than the myths and stories that are crippling to women, such as the creation myths that challenge our inherent knowledge that we are divine creations.

Reliving Eve's responsibility for the downfall of humanity by way of a piece of fruit has made too many women accept from the get-go that they are blemished and stained – that they are flawed. Many women believe they can never feel empowered because of this story, but it's only one among many told over and over again. This, in itself, is a point that should be interesting to the neurophysiology movement, because it says something about the power we have as a group consciousness.

When an entire society believes something negative, and those thoughts permeate our own brains, reinforcing automatic programs within our minds, we become truly unconscious as humans. The power from the outside may be so difficult to overcome that we finally give in and become sedated. It's just easier to surrender to massive group thinking than to fight it, generate awareness, and wake people up. The ones that do resist are usually labeled heretics and we execute some of them. It is unfortunate that we wear so much violence on the sleeve of our past.

As we learn more about our brains, and the capability we have to change our thoughts and the world, the past is not so frightening. We can stop falling prey to massive amounts of self-defeating thoughts from the past. We can revisit those thoughts objectively, learn from them, and distance ourselves from the emotion associated with that past event; then we can move forward by living in the present. Women, as well as men, can create newer group thought patterns that serve the greater good and that are much more reflective of today's roles. Things are beginning to move that way as women are starting to realize they are beautiful and whole images of creation.

We don't believe we are divine. Feeling empowered is about creating reality the way you see fit. But to exist in a positive state of exchange with your environment, you must recognize the Divine within. You already carry God or the spirit-power within, and it is your empowered state of being. It's what allows you to make changes to create a new reality. In order to change your life, you must believe it wholeheartedly. You are not some subset of the

Divine, or of someone else. You are fully and completely an individual spark of divine power. You *are* God.

Religion has had society in a conundrum over this idea. As a consequence of politics and power plays when scriptures were assembled, we've somehow cultivated messages of fear and self-doubt over our own God-self. Many people believe they must surrender their lives completely, abdicating the human experience in favor of a specific set of rules or religious dogma created by an outside, higher power who chooses for them. They have forgotten the power of their own mind and of the choice they have in making their lives a participative, creative endeavor with God. They favor the rules rather than following their own heart. Many believe that if they don't select the right channel, an eternal life of damnation awaits. It doesn't sound too nurturing.

Women cannot realize their true power, which is the power of being co-creators in their own lives, if they accept old religious doctrine that doesn't say anything positive about being female. If women truly believe they are less divine than men, how will they ever accept the idea that they are capable of being full participants in creating a world that reflects their values, hopes, and dreams? There will always be a reason why they *can't* succeed. It's old mental programming that needs major surgery.

Often, religion works wonderfully for men. Since today's mainstream religion does not embrace a female deity, God is clearly labeled "He" even though many ancient religions saw divinity differently. In our culture, He is perceived to be more powerful than She. Many outdated religious messages linger, translated into policies, laws, and family values that send messages to women that they are far less important than men. Most women are not raised with any images of a female god or female saviors, nor are they told there is a sacred part of the All that can be thought of as feminine. It's not a very empowering condition. So when we think women can't be happy, it may well be that they have accepted that their thoughts can create a reality for themselves, but when they attempt to practice that reality, they can't cross the final bridge to believing they are truly divine because society and religion tell them they aren't. There is a lot to be undone in that respect.

Women are complexity managers and overwhelmed with life in general. They wear too many hats, leaving little time to contemplate their own spiritual inheritance: their knowledge of who they are and where their power is seated. Nor do they find the time to *practice* it. What would help? Women need to stand up and admit they *are* divine, as an image of their creator. They need to celebrate their spiritual inheritance in spiritual practices that make sense to them and that integrate their intuitive natures. These are some of women's special needs in creating their own reality.

Remember, to be divine means we have assumed our divine state as creators who orchestrate our own reality. We are in charge of what we experience, and we can create anything out of our own manifested thoughts. The world, seen from this viewpoint, is a playroom, a laboratory, a practice ring, a place to try out and see what feedback we can obtain from what we think. We can make the world fabulous or we can destroy it. We have a choice to do either, as we have power to do anything we want. There's nobody telling us how to use our gift of self within the world we inherited. It's up to us.

Women have a tough time with this empowering thought because they don't see themselves in images of God. The divine feminine principle was squashed and reformatted as religions adopted a male-referent system, a system that still has a strong influence upon a woman's self-image. Challenging religions and finding a structured spirituality that reinforces women's values and recognizes women as individual sparks of the Divine seem like big hurdles to overcome. But they are the final barriers between a woman's creation of her own reality and her stepping into it in the form of her life.

WHY SHOULD WE GROW OUR GODDESS WITHIN?

Reviving an image of the Goddess can bridge this conceptual gap for women, because it helps them to see themselves in the face of the Divine. The Goddess becomes an entity they can relate to, someone who affirms their worth. They don't have to give up Father God to do it; they just need to acquire new knowledge on the subject of the feminine principle and integrate Her in their images of a spirit-power. Long ago, this was all very normal in female-oriented religions. It made spirit more accessible.

The reason we are living unbalanced lives, and seeing an unbalanced world culture, is that we do not recognize a balanced image of divinity. This imbalance has even affected the men who created the policies and the religions. So we cannot complete our thought process to produce what we want in our lives, unless we recognize that we are all divine, both men and women. For those who can't jump directly to a genderless image or concept, we need to revive Mother God to get us over the gap. God can be represented as a Mother/Father God. It's not a new idea!

The Gnostics, a sect of early Christians, conceived of God as a triune: Father/Spirit; Mother/Psyche-Soul, or the physical aspects of our existence; and Christ consciousness, who was the spirit embodied in the physical. Our job, according to the Gnostics, was to *become* a Christ, who created reality through thoughts. He didn't do it by falling out of the sky in some sort of invisible, ethereal body, waving a magic wand. The story of Christ exemplifies that there is a way to access your spirit-power within. It is *not* accomplished through denying your body or your individual soul – as a way to honor your individual expression of spirit – but by *embracing* body, spirit, and soul simultaneously and with passion.

We are born in the flesh with an opportunity to create reality by how we think. And by embracing the significance of the Mother Goddess, who is a reminder of our body, the earth, and our emotions, we are consciously aware of the responsibility we have to maintain our systems in balance. She gives us a world to manipulate. In doing so, we utilize our vehicle of power, which is our brain. It is an acceptance of our own divinity. With conscious awareness, we can become a channel for our spirit-power. And *that* is the true state of empowerment.

What This Book Can Do for You

The seven spiritual lessons in this book present ways in which we achieve access to a greater and more productive mental state. There's not a lot of theory. My lessons are fairly lighthearted because we need to keep our sense of humor about the process of living. We're going to make mistakes. It's why we're here! But we can unpeel each layer together and examine the rich and robust fruit of who we are.

Some lessons you will find familiar. Perhaps others have already pointed out ways in which you have developed negative programming. You will discover the source of negativity and reset your thinking to reprocess your experiences positively. Overall, these lessons allow you to take a closer look at ways to develop more personal power, leading to a healthy and balanced life.

How the Lessons Are Organized

My seven spiritual lessons are called **Insight**, **Balance**, **Resiliency**, **Your Authentic Self**, **Abundance**, **Corporate Soul**, and **The Divine Feminine**. Each directs you to find the source of old hurts within yourself, your family, your relationships, and your everyday home life. You will look at how to overcome adversity by embracing spirit within, and how to manage change to stay strong. For those of us who reject the status quo, I reinforce why we should treasure being different and rely upon knowing our true self, and not our image as reflected in others. A lesson in abundance thinking will help you unseat negative past programming about money and form new attitudes to yield financial success. For women who are part of organizational life, a lesson reminds you to guide your workplace efforts by appreciating feminine values, helping you experience personal growth, both inside and outside the office.

As you journey to the seventh lesson, you have an opportunity to unseat old negative programming about being a woman.

If we attempt to change a negative thought but forget about accepting that we are spirit, then our brain can't fully accept our new belief. It's a package deal. In the seventh lesson, by affirming that your true self is a construct of both God and Goddess power, a constant source of strength, you can magnify your own sense of what it means to be a fabulous individual filled with light and positive energy, lovingly connected to everyone.

In each lesson, I share my spiritual perspective along with comments from women who are just like you. Each lesson ends with **Taking Spiritual Inventory**: a series of questions to help you **analyze** where your blockages reside, then **affirm** what you want to become permanent in your life with a positive statement. In **Walk the Talk**, I encourage you to list actions and realistic changes that will help you achieve a new set of goals. Finally, if you belong to a forum, sacred circle, or discussion group, you can share your personal strengths and strategies, putting your new awareness into practice. We learn to **share the spirit** by allowing others to help us create and stick to new changes. In the process of healing others, we heal ourselves.

For more affirmations that will help you reprogram your mind and get you on the path to creating new neural networks, I have written a companion book called *The Women's Book of Empowerment: 323 Affirmations That Change Everyday Problems into Moments of Potential*. It's a quick way to find the source of your stress, anxiety, or negative thinking and quickly readjust. Use it in conjunction with *Let Your Goddess Grow!* With these two books, I know you will be able to make better sense of life.

Move Forward and Know That All Is Well!

Remember, we can survive, but we can always do better than that: we can create reality. There really doesn't seem to be any other way to live. How healthy can it be to choose to stay underneath piles of loss, disappointment, grief, and old family resentments? There is only one way out, and that is to dust off your boots and climb out. I will help you take the first step and find courage, energy, and inspiration in the process. Together we can become modern female beacons of light, guiding even the most demanding curmudgeons we encounter.

Above all, know that we are beautiful entities – and the soul's journey is a gift, a miracle. We are beloved treasures who have an incredible opportunity to learn. People who are our greatest critics are there for our own benefit. By harnessing our own capabilities to create a world where we express our own divinity, we can evolve together. And who knows where it will lead? Consciously engaging in the process of true self-discovery will certainly give us more comfort in knowing we are meant to be here, exploring our limits. With a light heart and a good attitude, we will find it easy to share our wisdom and insight with others on the same work path. We just might find a bit of humor in our daily journey and, yes, even love for those around us who are helping to refine our soul. My greatest wish is that you can join me in thanking them for allowing us yet another opportunity to grow.

Goddess Blessings,
Charlene M. Proctor, PhD

WE GAIN INSIGHT BY
ALLOWING CHANGE IN
OUR LIVES AND LETTING
GO OF THE PAST.

Insight

Gain Insight by
Examining the Past

How Do We Gain Insight?

*I take the most chaotic moment of
the day and go deep to center myself.*

– Jane, nurse

The time we spend on earth is very short when you consider the scope of the universe. Often, we don't see the big picture and get lost in the details. What is our purpose in the few years we have? It is to become a living embodiment of spirit while we are here. We must learn to express spirit through our actions, emotions, and relationships and in the work we do, which can be anything from loving our children to being a bank teller. We're supposed to nurture one another, love the planet that provides us sustenance, evolve our soul in the process, then go home, perhaps to try another version at some later date. There's no single instruction manual for this type of big-picture thinking – to a large degree, we make it up as we go along. Being born is like standing on the bank of a big river and jumping into an already moving stream of people and events, all colored by the past – the past that others have left behind, but mostly the past that we create during our stay.

The past is important because we learn from it. The past helps us navigate through our current choices in order to evolve our soul. We're in soul school from the minute we hit the ground until we cross over; it's coursework made possible by the enriching and sometime challenging conditions we have chosen. We chart a learning program well before we get here, which includes our parents, our gender, and circumstances that will provide us with the greatest opportunity for personal and spiritual growth.

Where we get into trouble is in giving up our freedom to make new choices based upon the *present*. Every day is new, no matter how you slice it. The sun comes up in spite of our mistakes or the despair we must face. But we are meant to continually move forward. Getting stuck in the past holds us behind, as prisoners within an incredible universe of opportunity. True empowerment stems from living *now*, not reacting to now from a mindset of the past or living with worry about what might happen tomorrow, next month, or next year. Every day, no matter what has happened to you in the past, is a new opportunity to begin painting your life on a fresh, new canvas.

Begin to Set a New Mental Agenda

Some may argue that my philosophy is unrealistic since we just *can't* make life up as we go along. You've been taught that life is serious: plan for disaster, be prepared, and anticipate what might be coming around the bend. After all, there could be a calamity on the way. I'm not referring to the concern you give to the future of your financial portfolio or what your children will be doing in school next week. I mean carrying over negative programs from the past, those deep-seated, negative thought patterns that deplete our energy reserves and diminish our ability to make a difference in the lives of others *today*.

How many of you have heard people say, "Life is hard, a daily struggle." How about "If you don't have your health, you don't have anything"? If you don't have excellent health, yes, things might be fairly bleak, but there still is an awful lot of life to be had. Life has many meanings but often we've got the definition backwards. As an exchange with others, life isn't all about taking it in. It's mostly about what you give out.

This I know to be true, based upon my observations of many people who are critically ill yet have fantastic attitudes about sharing themselves with others. If you visit a pediatric cancer ward, you will see children who are physically challenged beyond words but are still an inspiration to everyone around them. Despite their prognosis, their light shines bright with hope because they are living one day at a time. They seem illuminated and, thankfully, keep the rest of us going. Quite frankly, they are among the most inspirational people we have on earth, because they make everyone stop and think, "If life can be good despite those circumstances, then why am I holding myself back?" I believe part of their purpose is to give the rest of us a wake-up call to change our outlook. And if we find ourselves in the same boat, we too can keep everyone else going strong while we test our own abilities to stay in the present moment.

Depending upon how you were raised, you might even have been told, "Life is tough, you get old, then you die." Good grief, who thought this one up? Yet I have seen people carry this type of negativity on their sleeve, using it as a battle cry to justify every bad circumstance they encounter because they don't expect life will get any better. If you don't believe things will improve, then why in the world would they? I believe we set a mental agenda every day, and what we see in our world and our personal lives is a result of what we think. If you aren't getting what you want out of life, then you must create a mental discipline that replaces a negative belief system with one of hope, appreciation of the past, and a decisive statement of what you see happening in the present. The present is what matters.

WE ARE CHEMICAL BEINGS

Many people think they have little control over their circumstances. They believe their external environment determines their lives. But the truth is that humans have the ability to produce the effects they want in the world simply by observing themselves from another point of view. We have the ability to choose the way we react to people and circumstances because we can override old, ingrained patterns in the brain that are no longer useful.

Scientists have determined that we hard-wire our own brains, for the most part, by our associative memory: our associations with people, events, times, places, and things. We assign emotions to the memories recorded in those complex strings of nerve cells wired together; the strings become networks of information we can access automatically at any time. Connections between our nerve cells are strengthened when repeatedly stimulated, in a process called "long-term potentiation." Through associative learning, our brains are programmed not only by ordinary experiences but by extreme circumstances. Trauma actually changes the structure and function of the brain.

We rely upon automatic programs of many kinds to help us function. Neural networks give us an opportunity to shift into cruise control – we don't have to think about typing, we just type. We've established the network by repetition.

But thoughts affect our bodies. As we work at living positively in the present moment, not in the past, our automatic programs can become problematic. We may have patterns set in place that do not serve us well. Our response to some new stimulus in our environment, such as a person, a relationship, or an event, could be based upon old information. Reactions to old experiences, such as despair, low self-esteem, or even pleasure from eating can become ingrained as patterns in our brain because those emotions produce chemicals that give us a boost. Every emotion we feel circulates through our bodies as chemicals called neuropeptides. The neurobiologist Candice Pert suggests that these short-chain amino acids or proteins talk to every cell of our body through receptor sites, guiding our perception of our choices. When our receptor sites are repeatedly bombarded by the same neuropeptides, they begin to crave them. In other words, our bodies become addicted to our emotional states, whether good or bad. If you are repeating the same relationship patterns, for example, it means that your body has developed a chemical appetite for those experiences. Like an addict, you'll draw experiences toward you that give you a fix.

However, we are born with the ability to change our networks. Our brains are actually very adaptable. Neurons are inherently regenerative and flexible, so we are able to rearrange the connections between them throughout our lives. We can break unproductive patterns of memories and prevent our nerve cells from forming connections. It's called pruning. No longer will new experiences activate the old automatic programs. Your perception of relationships or events can change.

Through awareness of your automatic programs developed from the past, you have the ability to change your circumstances. When you change the way you react, new thoughts create new systems in the brain, which produce new chemistry associated with an emotional exchange. Interrupting the programs weakens the connections in the brain, neuron by neuron. It's like breaking a habit. You can choose to override the impulse to feel a certain way and decide to react differently to life.

If the same things keep happening in your life – for example, you keep recreating the same type of relationships or experiencing the same conflicts at work – your perception of those external circumstances never changes. If you can't live without those old thought patterns, you'll never perceive the world in a new way, creating new experiences and expectations. Your external environment is giving you feedback that there's something wrong with your thinking. But, if you choose, you can change.

The first choice in creating a new life is to cancel those old programs, which will disrupt the strings of neurons firing together. As we develop more skills and tasks giving us the ability to act automatically in new ways, we construct a fresh set of neural networks. When the body accepts the new ideas, which is a natural and simple thing for the body to do, we function differently. The value we get out of life, in the form of our interaction with the world, is a positive and loving experience.

In order to live joyfully and master difficult situations, we must overcome old impulses we've had for years. We want to align our thought processes to new ideas and give up the comfort from emotions that are familiar but no longer serve our higher good. We want to develop new outlooks that allow us to base our reactions in the present, not the past!

EMOTIONAL CARRYOVER

Changing a negative outlook takes a bit of discipline because you have to deeply resonate with the idea of what you want in the present moment, and accept it as already happening. When you attune to an idea, goal, or state of mind, you want to attract it *now*, not in the future. And it takes a lot of self-love.

Do some simple mental housecleaning to discover if what you are feeling now is being embroidered upon by the past. If you're discouraged, shift your thinking to the "today" setting and stop dredging up all sorts of feelings from the last twenty years – about your parents, jobs that no longer matter, or even people who let you down. Release those people and circumstances and be free. If you carry so much heaviness from the past, you'll never get out from under water. The past is over. Do yourself a favor and lighten your load – buoyancy guaranteed.

PAULINE'S STORY

I have a friend whose parents were divorced while she was young, leaving her with a heavy dose of low self-esteem, feelings of abandonment, and a lack of a positive self-image. That experience makes her feel incomplete without a man, and since her own difficult divorce seven years ago, she continues to believe that a loving relationship will complete her as an individual and prove her to be lovable and worthy. In the last two years, every relationship she has had has ended because her expectations of what another individual can bring to her life are so huge that no person could possibly meet them. Her problem is not with the expectation; it is with the belief system underlying the expectation. She wants to attract a loving relationship, her "one true love," but she does not truly believe that she is worthy of love, and she brings the past as a vessel to be filled first. Her emotional state is cluttered with loneliness and unhappiness.

> I think women love to talk and express their feelings. I think women have a verbal communication need. In my opinion, men don't seem to need quite as much of that.
>
> *Elaine, attorney*

Not long ago, I asked her if she could take a minute to think about the big picture and refocus her intentions. I asked her to think for a moment about the concept of divine love. We cannot ever be filled as deeply or completely by any human being as we are filled with the divine love of spirit, or our source, which is also our higher self at work in our lives. We must first love our authentic self deeply, believing our gifts are magnificent, and know we are never alone. It is impossible to be alone because we are constantly channeling spirit though everything we do. It is also impossible to be unloved, because if you love yourself, you are releasing those gifts from the source, which is made of pure love. At that abstract level, your source and your self are essentially the same.

In life, we are supposed to demonstrate that love. It is natural for us to do so because it is part of our divine heritage. In doing so, we are being loved and also loving ourselves. That's the potential for a whole lot of love to participate in at any given moment, even without another person to send you flowers and greeting cards. In the big picture, you're participating in a loving, co-creative exercise between spirit and the manifested world. *That* love is the ultimate, and once you get it, you will attract so much love in your life that you will be overwhelmed with how many ways it comes to you.

Has my friend subscribed to that idea? No, but I'm still working on her. She tells me she could not possibly forgive her ex-husband for being a terrible partner. She continues to shop for a relationship that meets her needs and I am still talking about self-love, and the release of negative past programming as a prerequisite to leading a balanced life.

FEAR AND SELF-DOUBT

I think we are often fearful of believing we can have anything we want. When we look at the world, we see so much lack, unhappiness, war, starvation, pain, struggle, limitation. We begin to believe in it, and then we give those ideas power. With the number of people we see every day immersed in those conditions, it seems nearly impossible to trust that the normal human experience can be one of abundance, joy, peace, fulfillment, health, and ease. We've been told since childhood that "nothing's perfect." Nothing is worse than this type of programming, because we're never going to realize our full human potential until we release our former ideas of what is possible. Life is a beautiful, perfect, glorious miracle. We choose our situations, our families, our painful experiences in order to evolve.

As we observe the full range of everything from despair to triumph, we see the huge opportunity that exists to make change. Despair challenges our perception of what *can* be. With fear and self-doubt in our toolkit, our capability to produce change is diminished. In the big picture, life *is* perfect because it is giving us room to grow. A little bad weather makes us sturdier. We need the rain, and even a cold winter solidifies us, making us more receptive to spring. But, sure as anything, we *are* going to grow despite our circumstances. There should be no fear of growth. We should be proud of surviving, overcoming, beating the odds, not living in fear of more to come, and especially proud of not dragging ourselves down, together with those around us, with emotions like fear and self-doubt that do nothing but keep us in the dark.

Classify the Past

What is the past? It is a collection of our emotions, experiences, and thought patterns as a result of living life. As adults, when we feel an emotion, it's often based upon past experience. Life events trigger our emotional collection, and we interpret our current experiences through this lens. The problem is the value we take away from the past. When we allow only the good to shine through, we are able to live in the present. When we worry about the future, or agonize over the past, we are not fully engaged in life. The trick is to stay focused on your capabilities to address the present. View your past as a wonderful, robust course in life and stop agonizing over your mistakes, your parents, or what someone said.

> We need to be happy with ourselves and accept who we are.
>
> *Donna, salesperson*

Expect the Best and Know the Universe Will Creatively Respond

Negative programming stems from messages we receive as children from those who are closest to us. If you had parents who believed in lack, who were sure that life could never be fun and that you never get what you want, then by the time you left home you already had a personal philosophy that permitted you to be disappointed in life. If that is what you expected, then why would the universe ever give you more? If we are responsible for creating our own happiness, then we'd better make sure we start off with a pretty grand vision of what happiness can be. Then we can go for it, and not expect it to magically happen. It won't happen unless you expect it.

There's an old saying that I'm certain you've heard: "Be careful what you wish for – you might get it." This is contrary to how the universe works. The universe provides you with anything you want and need. But even if you revise that statement to "Be careful what you wish for – you *will* get it," you reinforce the certainty that you will receive something, eventually. If you keep affirming this, then the universe will provide you with exactly what you want – all at a later date, which will always be in the future, not now. You'll never see it.

Anyway, why should we be careful what we wish for? This cautious statement implies that we may not deserve the wish, because we doubt our ability to use the wish wisely. Also, saying we "might" receive something sounds as if we really don't trust that our desires will be met. Not a very empowering thought.

What we ought to be practicing (and teaching everyone!) is the visualization of what we want, followed by the affirmation that we are already in receipt of it. Be open to a limitless world of opportunity, make up your mind, be decisive, say what you want, and be perceptive when that goodness comes into your life. Your wildest wish may come true in the form of an opportunity, not necessarily a winning lottery ticket. Give the universe a license to be creative. A positive statement based in the present would be something like: "I am a magnet for financial success. I am enjoying my wish because I attract success and opportunity wherever I go. I love being successful and having money because it means I create more opportunity for others. Having money is fun!" Remind yourself, and others, that you can bring whatever you want into your life, as long as you set your mind to it and believe wholeheartedly it is already here. Keep your intention clear about what you want, without attachment to the outcome, and you'll see wonders manifested in your life.

Negative programming is very powerful because it limits your vision of what you can have today. To produce positive change, you must take inventory of old, negative, and useless assumptions about life. How many times have you adopted past programming that has limited your thinking about what you can do? See if any of these statements can provide insight on what you expect from life.

You can't do that: girls just don't do that.

Children should always take care of the parents.

You have to make me happy, I sacrificed everything for you.

This family comes first, not you.

We just don't talk about those things.

You don't deserve to be loved.

I'm poor but good.

The world is a terrible place.

You'll fail/get hurt/be taken advantage of, so don't try.

Life stinks.

I don't have to apologize because I'm the parent.

You make enough mistakes and you'll learn how hard life is.

I knew that relationship wouldn't work out for you but you just didn't listen.

You'll never make any money doing that, so why bother?

What's the point of going to school when you have someone to take care of you?

By the time we launch into the world, we are by-products of the messages of institutions and other people – our parents, teachers, friends, relatives. We then create our present with a full palette of ideas that are not truly our own! Let's re-educate ourselves with some mental housecleaning.

EXERCISE: UNEARTHING OLD IDEAS

Plow through your field of negative assumptions about life along with the emotions that turn up with them. What negative messages do you think you have carried over from the past?

Negative Assumption	How It Makes Me Feel
_____	_____
_____	_____
_____	_____
_____	_____
_____	_____
_____	_____
_____	_____

Shed your attachment to ideas that hold you back from achieving what you want. To stay centered in the present, you'll need to stop investing energy in grumbling about what's happened, and instead find comfort in believing that every negative circumstance contributes something to your higher self-development. This will give you peace of mind about how you've arrived at today. Your soul journey will always unfold with surprises, both good and bad, and your challenge is to embrace it at all levels of experience. Learn to move forward with a sense of accomplishment and know, deep inside, that the very core of your spirit is waiting to be put to good use.

Consciously Create Your Day

Over the years, I have experimented with ways to release the past and move forward, living life in the present moment. I've noticed that when I start my day without any clear direction of how I choose to think, I don't get the results I want. I used to spend years regurgitating old problems. Without establishing my expectations of the universe as to how I desired my day to unfold, I discovered I would replay those same issues over and over again. So I began to make a supreme effort to move disappointments, loss, and feelings of non-success farther from my mind each day.

Now, before I get up in the morning, I lie in bed for a few minutes and create my day by using a series of affirmative statements that are designed to do three things: they are positive, present-moment statements about what is, not what will be; they address some element of my life that needs improvement; and they get me to completely identify with the power within to manifest my circumstances. To manifest means to bring into our immediate experience, and make that which is created by the mind into a tangible or observable reality. The power is derived from spirit, or the Divine, which pervades every inch of the universe. To achieve this goal, I say my affirmative statements with love, grateful to be alive and to have my chosen learning opportunities. Then I focus on being open to positive change.

I also visualize the perfection of life being unfolded to me in creative ways. I ask the universe to show me its perfection in ways

I would not expect. I make a point of saying this because I think we can better understand the co-creative relationship we have with spirit when we release our intentions and let the power of our own thoughts return to us in ways that give us feedback on our desires.

When I began to consciously create my day, it took at least a week to quiet the chatter in my head. I'd set my positive statements into motion and my mind would immediately argue that this wasn't the way we'd been doing things for so long. Thoughts about yesterday, 10 years ago, what my web developers did, feeding the dog, who needed a ride to school, and old hurts bubbled up in the form of images and feelings attempting to override my new thinking. If you've experienced the same, you'll know it's proof of the work necessary to release old programs. But gradually I found it easier to bring my attention to the present moment, to get quiet enough to invite my body and mind to a field of information, so I could fully accept it. It took three weeks.

On the days I did well at setting my intentions for the day, I noticed tremendous effects, especially when my intentions were broad. For example, some days I would open myself up to channeling spirit through my work or writing. Through constant awareness (pulling my thoughts back into alignment with those ideas throughout the day) I had amazing feedback. New people would walk in off the street and become my employees because I saw needs to be filled in our organization. I've had abundance arrive in the form of revenue streams I did not expect. When I consciously created my day, I saw results. A big part of conscious awareness, and living in the present moment, is about being open to the feedback the environment is providing. Be perceptive!

While I was learning to clear old and useless mental clutter, I found myself regularly using affirmative statements. Here are a few.

FEAR

I release all fear from my physical body. I am unafraid of the future because I am part of a divine plan to cultivate my self-development. Any change in my life is met with grace and dignity. I welcome the opportunity to show others how to navigate through difficult situations without losing hope. My natural state of being is love, not fear. I reset my mental and emotional perimeter to surround this situation with divine love. I rely upon a higher power to make me stronger. It is impossible for me to attract negativity because only love can permeate my surround. Today I exist in a spiritual womb that nurtures and protects me.

FORGIVENESS

I forgive because I am capable of expressing compassion. By forgiving, I release this situation from my energy field and feel clear-headed and full-hearted. I forgive because I am able to rise to my higher self and feel lighter. My light knows no boundaries when I forgive. Life feels lighter when I forgive.

REPEATING SAME PATTERNS

I keep experiencing the same events in my life because I have not learned a lesson at the deep level of the soul. I am committed to changing my behavior, attitude, and negative belief systems. I learn from past mistakes. Life is a self-educational process and I am a perceptive individual. I watch others as they model what I need to learn. I love all my talents as well as my imperfections, because that is what makes me the beloved person I am.

For more affirmations, see my companion book, *The Women's Book of Empowerment: 323 Affirmations That Change Everyday Problems into Moments of Potential* (The Goddess Network Press, 2005). Available through any major online book retailer or www.thegoddessnetwork.net.

Taking Spiritual Inventory: How Do We Gain Insight?

Analyze

Check your emotional barometer. List barriers to your happiness and divide them into two sets: *Red Light* (immediate concern!) and *Parking Lot* (to deal with later). When making the list, ask yourself:

* What is my current state of mind and heart? What do I think? How do I feel?
* Are elements of my personal life (past and present) interfering with my ability to communicate in a positive way with my friends, family, partner, or colleagues?
* What triggers my negative thinking? Does it result in a lack of self-confidence? Do I doubt my abilities?
* What patterns recur in my life that I no longer welcome?
* What old assumptions can I release that are not for my higher good?
* What experiences in my life am I fearful of letting go?

Affirm

Release and overcome the past by affirming all good in your life. Write an affirmation that reminds you to stay in the present.

_____

_____

_____

_____

_____

_____

_____

_____

Walk the Talk

List the realistic actions you will take to heal yourself. What will you do to act?

_____

_____

_____

_____

_____

_____

_____

_____

_____

_____

_____

_____

_____

Share the Spirit

Let's share strategies to stay on the path to self-healing. What changes do you think can be made in the next two weeks? Share your strengths and weaknesses in overcoming the past. Discuss your ideas to move forward in life and techniques you might have already discovered to release the past. Consider the following topics for discussion.

* How do we manage the past and the present simultaneously? What happens when we bury the past? What spiritual principles should we employ to manage the past? (For example, forgiveness or trusting the universe.)
* Is it realistic to expect that others will think as you do? How do we move through life being "ambassadors of now"?

* What happens when we visualize a better today and begin to move forward? How do others react? Share your experiences in using affirmations with your group.
* How do the old thought patterns we carry manifest themselves in our home life, our personal relationships, and our careers?
* Is it possible to forgive anyone for any circumstance? Do we have different rules of forgiveness for others than for ourselves?

OUR LIVES ARE A COMPLEX
ROTATION OF CIRCUMSTANCES
THAT CAN BE BALANCED WITH
OUR OWN AWARENESS AND
OUR DESIRE TO NURTURE
OURSELVES.

Balance

Manage the Daily
Complexity of Work,
Family, and You

How Do We Manage Daily Complexity?

You almost need to be a superhuman to keep going,
to keep your best foot forward. Life is so demanding.

– Kerri, administrative assistant, wife, mother

The most dominant feature of modern life is the pace we attempt
to maintain. Compared with us when we were in school, our kids
have a multitude of information to process, resulting in longer
and longer days. It's the same for adults. The evening news is now
a simultaneous, multiple-station event. If we're not channel surf-
ing, we can settle on one network, but between the ticker tape at
the bottom of the screen, the main anchor, split screens, and going
around the world in eighty seconds or less – frankly, I'm mentally
exhausted after taking in the nightly whirlwind of viewpoints. It
is a reflection of how fast we expect to receive our information: if
we can't get what we want in less than a few minutes, we're on to
something else, or someone else, that can get it to us faster.

Thank goodness this has been the paradigm for the information age, otherwise we'd still be at our old mainframes in the office,
carting stacks of paper punch cards around instead of microchips.
The good thing is that humanity is better connected through technology. But the flip side is that it runs our lives and sets the pace,
sometimes so fast that we don't know whether to leap out of bed
another hour earlier to get it all done, or simply wear tomorrow's
clothes to bed so we can save fifteen minutes in the morning. Or
better yet, let's not go to bed at all. Didn't Leonardo da Vinci and
Buckminster Fuller train themselves to slide into polyphasic sleep
within minutes and snooze less than two hours a day? Perhaps we

should add this skill to the high school curriculum so our kids can adequately prepare for the world at large.

> American culture needs to slow down.
>
> *Sara, education administrator*

What we ought to do is regularly send them up a mountain to revisit life without television, pocket PCs, Palm Pilots, instant messaging, and cellphones. But then again, our kids would probably remind us that they can take their laptop computers up the mountain by way of wireless technology, so why not meditate in the middle of a few downloads off the Internet? We're so integrated with technology that hastens the pace, we might as well surrender to it. Given the choice, I'd bet we would opt for regular updates on what they're doing by way of digital photos, e-mailed home once a day.

STAYING GROUNDED

Everyone knows part of human nature is to connect with nature at a deep level – to appreciate the rhythm of life that existed before PDAs. Our community is much more than people, it's every living thing. Regrettably, there's no turning back to a simpler time. It's too late to resign ourselves completely to the mountaintop scenario; even Gary Zukav occasionally makes the trek down to be on *Oprah*. The new generation's challenge will be to learn how to maintain balance between our natural and technological worlds, and we are already being warned of what will happen if we don't find that balance.

Our society feels this uncertainty at a subconscious level because it is a recurrent theme in the films we see, which are such a huge part of American culture. In many ways, we are forecasting reality by creating it on-screen. The film industry is very good at giving us a peek at a possible future because we can stretch the limits of our imagination, both visually and thematically, along with a best-outcome scenario. Remember *The Matrix Reloaded?* Neo battles the residual effects and horrors of artificial intelligence run amok by developing strength in his mental, emotional, and spiritual focus. He finally understands his true source, knowing he is more than what he sees. His real energy reserve comes from within – that's what permits him to transform the world.

> I think things are going too fast, people are moving too fast without thinking. They try to get there first instead of trying to get there ethically, morally, and spiritually.
>
> *Lisa, charity director*

I think this is a wonderful image of the current state of the world and a lesson in how to stay grounded. Like Neo, we can operate in both the technological and the earth worlds to stay in balance, as long as we know life's challenges are an illusion. We had better maintain a spiritual focus through it all; otherwise, we will never know what it is worthwhile to expend our energy on. Society is beginning to seriously reinforce the idea that the fundamental glue holding life together is our spirit, our higher self. More important, when we go out into the world, we must rely upon our true self for strength and use it to separate what matters and what does not. Obi-Wan Kenobi, step aside. We've now relinquished our light sabers in favor of positive, spiritual energy, delivered to us by our contemporary film heroes. We finally have permission to overcome our difficulties in life with nothing more than a strong sense of self, a positive attitude, and love.

Let's transform the real world with these artistic visions by renewing our belief in spirit. Make spirit part of your day. A balanced life always begins with an unlimited reserve of divine energy. Perhaps we are helping to build a more balanced future by seeing what can happen when the sum of what we create is synergized with an awakening of spirit and becomes even greater. Using this skill set is a very big first lesson in managing complexity.

Women Are Natural Complexity Managers

Whether we are managing complexity in the office or at home, it is beyond reasonable doubt that women are the ultimate multi-taskers, the queens of complexity management. What makes us so capable? Many researchers have been tackling this one for years. They have reached consensus on a few items that have to do with the left brain (linear progression, logic, doing) and the right brain (gestalt, intuition, being). The left side of the brain deals with discriminatory skills and the analytic mode, while the right side deals with holism. Although men and women have the same basic brains and intelligence capabilities, women may be wired differently because of chemicals, hormones, and the density of certain brain regions.

Although it is scientifically inconclusive, plenty of evidence suggests that women may be designed to just process life differently. Why? Women activate more neurons in the brain. Women have between 10 percent and 33 percent more neuronal fibers than men in the forward part of the corpus callosum, the dense fibers that link the two hemispheres of the brain. Because they have more connecting neurons between left and right hemispheres, they tend to use both sides of their brain more than men when problem solving. The male brain tends to compartmentalize and divide tasks between its two hemispheres, suggesting that a man's ability to focus intensely may be due to the way his brain processes information. Although women can also focus on a single task like men, they are generally much more aware of their emotional depth and are able to perform multiple tasks simultaneously more often than men. In other words, the two sides of a woman's brain talk to each other. Women are naturally great at integration, communication, and seeing the big picture.

Women can list more than "plentiful brain fibers" on their résumés when applying for jobs in complexity management. Since women hear a much broader range of sounds, and use both ears more equally in listening to words, a woman's auditory skills enable her to plot a course through many conversations at the same time. Is it any surprise that we can all be talking at once and still know exactly what's going on?

In our eyes, we all have rods and cones, but women have far more rods in their retinas than men and therefore better peripheral vision, because rods make the eyes light-sensitive. Rods allow us to detect a slight movement in a visual field and let us see better in the dark in order to take in more at a glance. On the other hand, men have more cones than women. They can see one segment of the visual field in greater detail and with better depth perception than women. Cones allow us to intensify clarity and scrutinize something in a sequence. Rods let us see the gestalt, the big picture.

Aren't these wonderful reminders of a woman's capabilities? Today's translation: in problem solving, men are better suited to deal with one thing at a time while women take in complexity all at once. What the scientists don't tell you is this: when complexity is overwhelming, by design or default, women not only shift into autopilot to pick up the slack but tend to deplete their emotional inventory along the way. Women are wired to keep taking it all in and to view life as one big operating system. No need to apologize for the way we do things – it's just who we are. And there are no special categories of rods and cones that help women stay on top of complexity – unless, of course, we maintain balance by telling our brains to rely more on the left side.

When we start piling up the gender-based facts of our own nature, it is undeniable that women not only have beautiful, incredible brains but are genetically suited to steer through the complexity of work, family, and home life. There's a great scene in *White Christmas* where General Waverly informs Emma, the confident and sometimes meddlesome housekeeper, that he will court-martial her for sending all his suits to the cleaners at the same time, leaving him nothing to wear but his army uniform to attend a surprise reunion of his military unit. "Go ahead," she retorts, knowing that he'll have to show up wearing the uniform because that is what she wants him to do anyway. "I'll make my own decisions," he argues back. "I got along very well in the army without you!" "Well," she says, before she turns on her heel and heads out the door, "it took 15,000 men to take my place!"

I love that scene. It reminds me we often don't congratulate ourselves enough for our intuitive ability to navigate through life's complex levels. Nor can we rely on receiving appreciation from the many people whose lives we organize. What we could have more of is a little self-appreciation of our ears, rods, and cones, and the fact that we are biologically gifted to *be* 15,000 men when needed. Now more than ever, it is our time to pull out the stops on the multitasking we do in building careers, raising families, managing aging parents, running everyday home life, and having some fun and social life in between. Honestly, if our culture recognized women's inherent capabilities, we'd be basking in self-love and amazement at what we've actually accomplished. We could recognize that it is indeed our time, *and our job*, more than at any point in history, to keep things going at work and on the home front, while facilitating spirit in the process.

RIDE DAILY COMPLEXITY WITH MORE PRESENT-MOMENT AWARENESS

Managing complexity is different than managing old, negative thought patterns. Your goal is to unseat negative thought patterns, and not create a more extensive inventory of old ideas and emotions to manage. Because of the pace women choose today, we are naturally gifted at managing complexity, but we must not rely exclusively on automatic programs to get through the day, without any sense of self-love, nurturing, or awareness that we are consciously creating our day for our *own* self-development, and not for others.

Although automatic programs help us function and navigate through complexity (who has time to think about how to drive the car so the kids can get to school?), we can't rely upon them like robots. For joyful and fulfilling lives, we must make an effort to be conscious of what we are doing and why throughout the process, taking time to evaluate what produces feelings of satisfaction. When there doesn't appear to be any positive feedback from the environment, we reset to the conscious awareness channel. Without adding any additional complexity, what can women do between laundry and writing corporate reports that would gently bring our minds back to a sense of purpose and present-moment awareness?

Build Thankfulness into Your Spiritual Skill Set

Living in a continual state of positive thankfulness is so important when managing life's complexity. True thankfulness is gratitude for life's learning opportunities *and* for spirit being present to get the lesson to sink in. It is impossible for us *not* to sweat the small stuff – for women, there is no small stuff! It's tough to rise every day knowing that each circumstance we encounter is meant to keep us learning on our soul journey. It is easy to get lost in the details, but what we can do is counter the challenges with some skills in the appreciation category.

First, you must affirm your innate ability to manage complexity and simply feel good about having a built-in skill set that you can lean on. For example:

I can do anything I set my mind to.

I am strong enough to withstand any criticism that comes my way.

I navigate through this course with ease.

I'm a social octopus and have fun doing things with so many people.

I have the ability to see this situation through because I believe in myself.

I'm captain of my own ship and set sail anywhere I choose.

I live through this day with effortlessness.

I help people wherever I go by being an example of strength and wisdom.

I feel on top of the world with spirit, which knows no boundary.

I'm smart, competent, and wise.

I have great experience in this area and I move forward with ease.

The second skill is to affirm that spirit is a part of each day and every circumstance, and invite it to become part of your skill set, in whatever manner feels right to you.

I rely upon Mother/Father God to help manage this situation.

I feel content knowing that spirit helps to choose what is best for me.

God can tackle this situation and works through me.

I channel divine love to aid in this situation.

With each breath I take, I am blessed and supported by a higher power.

The Goddess gives me healing power for this situation.

I am expressing the light of Christ consciousness with every word I speak.

I am supported by the universe.

The third and most certain way to manage complexity is to live in a state of thankfulness for all you have. You may think this is difficult to do: how can we be thankful for traffic jams, lousy weather, lost dogs, and missing luggage? The answer is: widen your perspective. Being thankful extends beyond the thanking we do for material possessions, job security, or life accomplishments, which is easy. A thankful state of mind and heart pertains to the continual acknowledgment that, in each and every instance when you experience something much less than ideal, the experience is for your greater good. In doing so, you are relying on your higher power, and strengthening your connection to the Divine. For example:

I am grateful for this opportunity to learn more about my capabilities.

I thank the universe for showing me this situation so I can be more compassionate toward others.

I appreciate all the beautiful parts of my body because I am a wondrous creation.

I welcome this challenge in my life and am thankful I can inspire others.

Because of the family I have chosen, I am thankful to be even stronger than yesterday.

I receive all my good with a thankful heart and rejoice in my blessings.

My difficulties today allow me to cultivate wisdom. I am a wise soul!

Adopting this type of thankfulness puts you in the Super Bowl of big-picture thinking. You are not thanking the universe for giving you a bad circumstance, which will only generate more bad happenings. Instead, you are flourishing in a state of complete appreciation for what life has to offer.

Don't you always feel more inclined to give more to someone when they are enthusiastic and appreciative? Consider the times you have helped someone and have been overwhelmed with thanks. Didn't it make you want to give more? Like does attract like, despite what you've been told in the past. Although at a subatomic level, positively and negatively charged particles are attracted to particles with the opposite sign, and repelled by particles with the same sign, they are not a good model for our own behavior and attitudes. Our theory of the electromagnetic force does not account for the state of the heart. If you want to be a person who is appreciated, then continue to give unselfishly, thanking others for all they do. The same is true with the universe. Life provides exactly what we continue to acknowledge. You've got to learn to love life, be *in love* with life, at an intimate level. Anytime we acknowledge that life is good, we are entering a state of gratitude. Be thankful you have an opportunity to challenge yourself.

This is a discipline requiring practice. Write thanks to yourself, and to others, on a regular basis. Wherever you go, show up with a compliment. When you visit someone, bring something positive in the form of affection or caring. Tell your friends how much you appreciate their sense of humor or their graciousness, and never assume they don't need to be thanked. Write thank-you notes for dinners, gifts, and prospects you receive from all people in your life – your family, your partner, your children, and your business colleagues. When people receive your thanks, especially in written form, they take a little bit

> I think women are out of balance because they are not following their own heart, they are not listening to themselves. They're filling expectations of what society, men, and everyone wants them to be rather than figuring it out for themselves.
>
> *Bea, wife, mother, restaurant owner*

of your spirit throughout the day. Quit procrastinating and learn to get the words out of yourself. Once you learn how to do that, you will be amazed how that energy comes back to you.

Living in a continual state of thanks for being alive and well, and having a chance to improve the lives of others through your words and actions, turns negative situations around very quickly. By allowing life to happen *through* you, you offer your own unique thumbprint of the Divine. That is called living with joy. Thankfulness for the present is an element of almost every affirmation. Live in a continual state of thankfulness, express it in your words and actions, and you will be among the most beloved people on this planet. Without a thankful mindset, we do not have nearly as great an opportunity to explore the limits of our patience and our capabilities as loving individuals.

EXERCISE: SELF-APPRECIATION

Were you told, or have you told yourself, that you're not good enough, smart enough, slim enough, young enough? Let's rewrite all the negative messages about our capabilities and change them into positive statements, so we can release those limiting assumptions forever.

Past:
How You Put Yourself Down

Present:
Magnifying Self-Love

_____   _____

_____   _____

_____   _____

_____   _____

_____   _____

_____   _____

_____   _____

Let's move forward by appreciating ourselves. Think about what others tell you about all the things you do well and why, and write them in the present tense. Mentally catalog your talents, beauty, and intelligence, and all the other things you love about yourself, and turn them into statements of thankfulness. I'll get you started.

> I am thankful for my beautiful body because it gets me where I need to go.
>
> I love my sense of humor! I spread a lot of joy around.
>
> I am competent! I've made it through four degrees and still love to learn.
>
> I'm a great parent because I listen carefully to my children's needs.
>
> I love the way I can provide for my parents – I feel great about being generous.
>
> My spirit is so huge, I can fill up a room by just standing here.

Write a thank-you note to yourself. Be joyful when you write it – you are a gift to the world.

Dear_____

_____

_____

_____

Love, Me

CONSCIOUSLY CREATE YOUR DAY

To add to your ongoing efforts to consciously create your day, here are a few affirmations to use when managing complexity seems overwhelming.

TRAPPED IN HOME LIFE

I am connected to the larger human and spiritual community by my thoughts, wishes, feelings, and prayers; therefore I am never limited by these four walls. My higher self is guiding me to places and prospects that are part of my consciousness. New opportunities are already manifesting in my experience. I am an open window to a beautiful world, both inside and outside my home!

FEELING AS IF I'M ON A TREADMILL

Today I stop to smell the flowers. My life is about thinking and feeling and not all about doing. By taking care of me first, I enhance my contribution to others. I am strong enough to say no when I sense that my energies may be misdirected. I focus on choosing experiences in my life that contribute to my own spiritual development.

NO TIME FOR SELF

I deserve to have time for my own interests because I am a worthy soul. Today I take time to appreciate my magnificence by not watching the clock. I rejuvenate my spirit with my feelings of self-worth. I feel more balanced and powerful when I take time for my own enjoyment. From this day forward, I no longer give any power to being an empty vessel that lacks self-worth. I am filled with life's bounty, love being alive, and love spending time with me.

For more affirmations, see my companion book, *The Women's Book of Empowerment: 323 Affirmations That Change Everyday Problems into Moments of Potential* (The Goddess Network Press, 2005). Available through any major online book retailer or at www.thegoddessnetwork.net.

Taking Spiritual Inventory: Developing Skill Sets to Manage Complexity

Analyze

Look at the areas of your life requiring balance. Let's make a "Balance Sheet" by dividing a page into two columns: *Red Light* (critical) and *Parking Lot* (to deal with later). Go through the following categories and evaluate your everyday complexity.

* People: Am I giving certain people in my life too much energy? If so, who?
* Daily Work: Does my work life resonate with my spiritual needs?
* Career: Do I express my gifts in the work I do each day? Do those around me notice my talents?
* Self-Love: Am I receptive to appreciation from others? From myself? In what areas do I need more positive strokes?
* Overdoing: In what areas of my life do I experience the most stress?
* Negative Thinking: In everyday situations, what are my biggest opportunities to thwart negativity from others? How can I keep from spiraling down into negativity on my own?

How can you simplify your activities and streamline your attitudes? Highlight the areas that need work.

Affirm

Decide what you want from today and reset your priorities. Write an affirmation that reminds you to stay in balance when managing complexity.

_____

_____

_____

_____

_____

_____

_____

_____

_____

Walk the Talk

Create an action plan to nurture yourself while meeting the needs of others. What can you do to increase your own physical, mental, emotional, and spiritual energy reserves? List ways to stay grounded and find peace among chaos. What activities can you give up to find time for yourself? Is "self-nurturing" all about creating more activities to do something for yourself, or is it about having a nurturing state of mind? List actions you will take to increase your level of self-nurturing.

_____

_____

_____

_____

_____

_____

_____

_____

Share the Spirit

What strategies help you manage complexity? Consider the following topics for discussion.

* We all have the same twenty-four hours in a day, which is the greatest equalizer between all humans. Do you feel you are racing to get to the finish line with more than the next person (more things, success, career advancement, children)? If so, why? What can you do to slow down the pace?
* Share your strategies to stay in a deep state of thankfulness. Is it possible to be thankful for everything, even negative circumstances?
* Do you rely on spirit to manage everyday complexity? If so, how?
* Have women taken the term "multitasking" to a new level in society? Do women wear it like a badge of honor? Or is it a result of society's expectations of us? Does it have anything to do with a woman's own self-image?
* Discuss how the concept of "deserve" may have taken on a negative connotation for you, either from past negative programming or your own feelings of self-worth. Do women generally lack balance between deserving and giving? Share your own personal stories about these concepts.
* How can we connect with spirit when managing complexity seems overwhelming? Some examples are prayer, meditation, being at one with nature, self-loving actions, and expressing gratitude.
* Does staying in the present and releasing the past help to manage your expectations of others, or of yourself?

WE ARE EARTHBOUND IN
OUR PAINFUL EXPERIENCES,
BUT WITH THE HELP OF
OTHERS WE CAN REACH
HIGHER FOR OUR SOUL
DEVELOPMENT.

Resiliency

Become Stronger
Through Adversity

Is It Possible to Embrace Life's Contrasts?

In my opinion, women are natural survivors and protectors. We are Mother Bear. We can defend a cause. We are survivors.

– Mary, landscape designer

Adversity is a subject we are well versed in by the end of our time on the planet. It's impossible to subscribe to life, and all it offers, without experiencing setbacks, disappointment, hurt, or grief. I believe spiritual development is fueled by the difficult circumstances we encounter. Although we can learn a tremendous amount by just having fun, refinement of the soul comes from adversity. Loss is an especially tough part of daily living, whether of a job, a spouse, a contract, your confidence, or even your car keys. Loss gives us the deepest pain and some of the greatest challenges we will ever face.

Everyone experiences patterns of gain and loss from day one. There are few exemptions. Suffering and adversity arrive periodically in their own intense forms. The good news is that we make better sense of loss as we become more experienced at living, even if there seems to be little logic behind it. Over the course of a lifetime, we ask "Why?" more times than can be remembered. The not knowing why seems just as painful as the loss itself, but everyone shares the same questions. Why do four people I know, who are part of my life, have to die in one year's time? How come every time I seem to get a little bit ahead

> I feel like Sisyphus eternally pushing the rock up the mountain. Some days, I feel it's inevitable I'll be doing the same thing tomorrow and next week.
>
> *Lou Anne, business owner*

in the business, the rug is pulled out from under me? Why do colleagues or friends betray me? Is there anyone who will truly understand me? Love me? Why do I have to keep going through the same things over and over again?

When asking others for guidance, how many times have you been told, "Well, to take a few steps forward, you have to take a few steps back"? I would be a zillionaire if I had a dollar for every time someone has said this as a way to explain adversity. Not very empowering advice to give and receive! Surprisingly, it is so ingrained in our repertoire of things to say to others, or even to ourselves when life gets us down, that we readily accept that we're going to tread water no matter what we do. It seems we already recognize that in order to get ahead and survive life's difficulties, we have to take the good with the bad. And the bad is expected in pretty big doses – certainly just as much as the good. After all, shouldn't we anticipate setbacks so we don't experience more disappointment when life takes an unexpected turn? Let's quit passing this adage around and write new, empowered sayings that take into account the greater strength we develop as a result of adversity.

You need to remind yourself that adversity was probably invented to keep providing you with a new and mature perspective on other areas of your life. How else could you stockpile greater strength for the really big stuff? If you've had more than your share of adversity, then you've got enough strength left over to let someone else lean on you for a bit.

Developing resiliency is all about drawing new conceptual parameters around adversity. That is fundamentally different from expecting bad, which just invites more failure and loss. If we expect failure, that is precisely what we will see more of. We'll attract it. That's why we keep our positive outlook in check by continuing our mental housecleaning, reprogramming negative thought patterns, and releasing old baggage so those ideas do not cast a shadow on our present-day living.

A better, more empowered philosophy is based upon the *benefits of change*. Translation: adversity equals your change potential. Embrace change and you will soar higher, last longer, feel fuller. Change is part of your soul story – and you need to keep on affirming that you continue to evolve within adverse circumstances for the benefit of perfecting your soul. Taking charge of change is about evolution and growth – and it is a part of the program, whether we like it or not.

Change Your Outlook on Change

Make no mistake about it, change is challenging, whether it is conscious or unexpected. Viewing adversity as change, not loss or failure, is part of empowered and positive thinking. Humans develop resiliency through change, both physiologically and emotionally. It's necessary for all life forms to evolve. Change comes through many vehicles: some hit us hard, others are rather sneaky. But despite the challenges change brings, we know it is our natural state. It's inevitable – the world grows and we grow with it.

We are already designed to express sorrow, frustration, anger, and resentment, even to give up for a while – and most of us choose to explore these feelings. But we are also designed to have hope, recover, be stronger, and inspire others as a result of change. You are never alone because emotion gives us plenty in common. As a society, we are not yet Vulcans.

What makes one person survive loss triumphantly and turn it into positive energy, while another person in similar circumstances resigns? It has to do with our underlying assumptions about change. Two of my very dear friends have had double mastectomies after breast cancer. Losing body parts is devastating, and it's followed by the daily strain of not knowing whether you are still in remission. Yet one woman has forged ahead as a life-force warrior, focusing on the triumphs and wins of today. She doesn't look back. The other has difficulty moving forward; she has quit her job and is waiting for "something" to happen while in a self-imposed limbo. They've processed their information completely differently. Why?

It's because people want certainty before they decide to accept change. It's a natural reaction. A current cultural disease we suffer from is predictability dependence, reflected in our inability to accept change at a deeply personal level. It applies across the board to choices we make with our finances, careers, or relationships. Science, especially when applied to health issues, has given us a false sense of security. After all, it seems we've been able to control nature. We like to think we've cornered the market on predictability and good planning, when the truth is that we live in a time when prediction is more intuition and common sense than science.

To embrace change, we need to release the umbilical cord we think we have to outcomes of certainty. In other words, stepping off the cliff requires a huge amount of trust. Your fall will be broken somewhere at the right time. Believing that is what allows us to cope. It is the first step, unsupported by any scientific doctrine. And it's a big one.

No matter what science pronounces, whether in the form of a diagnosis, a prognosis, or a prediction about the environment, there is no sure thing. Science has already given us permission to accept truth with a margin of error in just about anything. There is *always* the possibility that something may exist, or not exist, despite what patterns indicate. It is useless to let scientific standards, or lack of proof, for that matter, hold you back. After a health crisis, job loss, divorce, or death, you will successfully navigate through change and elevate the quality of your life by knowing that *anyone* can beat the odds. There is evidence everywhere, not just from Christopher Reeve, Mattie Stepanek, or those whose stories you find in *People* magazine but from the dry cleaner, your third cousin, your own child. Let's pay attention to the real evidence, instead of looking for ways to prove that we can't make it or that the odds are just too great.

Adopting a new attitude about adversity requires big-picture thinking on the subject of change. Life, including spiritual development, can be seen as an upward spiral where we experience some of the same lessons over and over again. Is it because we just aren't getting what the lesson is telling us? Yes, but that's not the only reason.

We've deliberately put those circumstances in our soul charts in frequent doses to allow ourselves an opportunity to see how we've been progressing on the upward part of that growth spiral. Adversity is an inescapable indicator of how we handle the bumps. We are meant to become stronger and more insightful each time we get walloped. With each business obstacle, make a stronger commitment toward your goal of service to humanity; each time you grieve, become better at comforting others and showing compassion; after each funeral, return home knowing that life is a precious gift. All setbacks drive the point home on the one true certainty in life, which is that we must use our time wisely to make conscious change in the world. Change is designed to get us outside of ourselves and make us conscious of our place within a community of souls. Without change, there is no transformation. Change is good, making us stir the self-development pot a little faster.

It's also important to cast the concept of change in a wider time frame. Although we gain power from present-moment thinking (*here and now* is important, not the past), it is helpful to view adversity and change over many lifetimes. How could you possibly perfect your soul in just one time around? There is so much to learn, with so many shades of gray to experience. Extending our perspective to the universal time frame relieves the pressure we often place on ourselves to get it all right at once – and gives us more patience with ourselves and with the others we are hauling along for the ride.

Use New Metaphors to Expand Your Thinking

Rather than telling ourselves there's loss and disappointment right around the corner, a more empowering frame of mind and heart is to look at our soul story frequently through metaphorical thinking. Metaphors help us to bridge the gap between very complex ideas and reality, because *all* knowledge, no matter how generated, is the result of an interpretive process.

Researchers often use metaphors to create a shared meaning about processes or relationships between variables. They help define different aspects of a reality. For example, an organizational manager might have a leadership style like Patton (hierarchical, top-down, expects orders not to be questioned), or a company culture might be like a jungle (unpredictable, unseen danger, can't trust colleagues). Metaphors capture entire systems of ideas that sometimes make sense of the senseless. They can permit people a language that reflects an already formed relationship with the world, complete with assumptions. We should regularly revisit metaphors as a means of understanding our soul stories – metaphors that provide us a frame of reference for life change.

Ancient cultures embraced the metaphor of a Great Mother (Mother God, the Goddess, Mother Nature) as a life paradigm. She's had hundreds of different names throughout the ages and has appeared in as many religions and philosophies. Through recounting folktales, myths, religious rites, symbols, and architecture, we've learned that people long ago viewed their life as existing within the womb of the Great Mother, in a cycle of birth, death, and rebirth evidenced by the stars, the seasons, and the process by which they experienced the natural world. They were smarter than we think; there was no other way to make sense of the world. People consumed and were consumed. Survival depended upon an ability to adapt to change, because it was necessary to accept it as part of the cyclical process. Nature was a metaphor for living and the Goddess served as a referent system for what people observed in life, growth and abundance as well as death and renewal.

Securing a physical place in the world, with its tremendous opportunity for experiencing our emotions, was considered a sacred journey, filled with unexpected modifications. Everything on earth was cyclical. As women, we approached life within this cycle. Life was seasonal to the human species, and cycles represented our mental and physical evolution. The journey of the soul, in human form, was supposed to progress within this conceptual framework with robust emotional diversity and triumphs.

Unfortunately, of late we have been operating without any good metaphors for change. We still think we can dodge adversity without recognizing it as the barometer of our own self-development; consequently, we have lost much of our power as spiritual individuals. When it comes to life's adversity, we need to revisit metaphors such as Mother Earth and recapture these ideas, making room for them every day. Change is natural and expected. We are out of touch with life's natural rhythm, not just in tree-hugging, saving the whales, or simply slowing down. We've lost our ability to accept life and its most fundamental properties, including the connection with our source, who is in an eternal state of flux.

> Do we really control anything? Do the best you can, and get a good night's sleep. That idea kept me going for years.
>
> *Annie, wife, mother, jewelry salesperson*

No matter how we analyze it, life has unexplainable, miraculous rhythms. We need to *consciously* exist within that rhythm. To our ancestors, being out of sync surely meant a life without meaning, and that still applies today. Our world is much more stressful than the world of long ago. Hunger? Finding shelter? Finding the way home? Try providing jobs for 200 people whose families depend upon you for their livelihood and medical benefits when the economy takes a spin. Or live in a nation where peace is precariously balanced with inconceivable violence, where the threat of terrorism becomes a secondary consideration when traveling to the store. It would do us a world of good to examine the metaphors we use to run the world, as well as the ones we use to organize our daily mindset, and examine why we fight the concept of change so much.

As a society, our lack of metaphor usage to deeply internalize the concept of change has been part of our slow divorce from an organic level as well as a spiritual level. It would behoove us to revisit our ideas of adversity through a natural lens in order to more easily accept life's contrasts. Through advanced medicine, we've been able to improve our health and we no longer accept early demises. We want to extend our time here, and the quality of our health, as long as possible. It's a good thing; no one is advocating suffering. But we forget there is a season for all things, including our health, jobs, and even the people in our life, and seasons are a series of fluctuations.

Life is a revolving door. The tide comes in and goes out. Having resiliency through it all is largely about accepting change and recognizing that life's contrasts make it the beloved and rich experience we signed up for. They are what make it *interesting* and invite us to extend our boundaries past what we think we can give. Despite frequent bad forecasts, there's an opportunity to experience the widest range of emotions possible, as well as the sacred task to improve, to do right, to grow. That is what the ancients taught. Yes, grasshopper, it's possible to begin another day filled with hope and trust despite the unknown. But how?

Don't Make Deals to Find Meaning in Catastrophe

A wrong way to keep moving forward is to exploit negative expectations by making deals with your source. We toss bargaining chips to the Divine in order to explain the inevitable. In my own family, I have seen the fulfillment of negative expectations be read as lending meaning to fallout after a catastrophe, and I've seen this bargaining turned into an excuse for self-denial. During childhood, we are frequently told that making spiritual deals ("God, if you only do this, I'll...") is a way to cope with life. It may make us feel better temporarily but I believe it generates unnecessary restrictions and helps to fulfill negative expectations.

When I was a child, my uncle was terminally ill and suffered greatly in the hospital. My mother told me that my aunt had made a deal with God, asking Him to take Uncle Jack soon, to ease his suffering. In exchange, Aunt Marcella told God she would give up one of her favorite pastimes in the world: eating chocolate, which she adored. According to the family informational network, Uncle Jack then died and Aunt Marcella never touched chocolate again. She saw this as a loving tribute to him, a gift of herself in the form of a sacrifice that bought her some control over the situation.

Although denying herself chocolate for the rest of her life became a participative endeavor in obtaining the outcome she desired, it also served as a sad reminder of loss every time she wanted to enjoy sweets. She felt giving up the chocolate was the price to have her prayer answered – it was a binding spiritual agreement. I wondered what would have happened if she had lost her willpower and sneaked a couple of truffles on the side. Lightning bolts? Guilt? Would it have changed anything? Does setting expectations for ourselves that we might not be able to meet in exchange for a spiritual deal create a desired outcome? This was fairly confusing to me as a child, and I wondered where I ought to be checking on the rules for the dying.

Another time, my grandmother lay ill with stomach cancer in the hospital, and my mother told me that she and my father had prayed to facilitate her release into heaven because she had had such an unfortunate life. My mother said that they gave so much of themselves in this spiritual request that, as a consequence, it lent meaning to a string of employment disasters for my dad, who lost his job and his entire thirty-five-year pension, and was unemployed for well over a year after my grandmother died. In my mother's mind, this devastating loss that jeopardized their financial future was a result of giving a part of herself she believed could not be replenished – a result of asking for spiritual assistance. Had my mother actually hastened my grandmother's departure to end her suffering by trading away their security? Or did my parents create a space for more loss in their own lives?

Many years later, the president of the company where my father had worked at the time of my grandmother's death was indicted for embezzlement. The entire company went bankrupt as a result of years of bad management. Did my father's employment troubles begin because of circumstances beyond his control? Or did they result from my parents' vision, made manifest by their belief system?

We often look for meaning in the wrong places. Punishing ourselves to even up one person's suffering with another's does not serve any purpose. We already share someone's suffering through compassion or through actions that ease their situation. By trying to make deals with the Divine, we are setting into motion an invitation to the universe for more strife – we expect and welcome it. And when it arrives, we acquiesce and allow it to become part of our lives through deprivation.

When someone is dying, why do we believe we facilitate the crossing-over process by emptying ourselves of that which sustains us and allows us to enjoy life to its fullest? Why do we think the Divine wants a demonstration of lack in our own lives as a consequence of someone else's death? By making deals, you are essentially negating life's natural course and attempting to take responsibility for another person's chosen method of departure.

We all choose our departure dates and methods of leaving before we get here. It is a necessary part of the soul chart – otherwise, life would be completely random and a result of luck. Why would some people get preferential treatment and others have to suffer terribly? The Divine does not dispense uneven justice, issuing a fantastic life to some and not to others. The soul that takes a lot on at once in the form of a challenging life has made a choice. Admire these people for being so brave!

Let's start to assign some positive meaning to crossing over. What we ought to be praying for, and affirming in such circumstances, is a swift journey home for the soul. When someone is about to cross over, we can't possibly know what we can give up, other than old baggage that will get musty after their departure. Let go of resentments and guilt. Release that person by visualizing them in a state of utter completion – they are going *home*. We should be thankful to have been part of their journey. And if the relationship has not been as good as we wanted, then ask for peace, insight, and strength to come your way, knowing you did the very best job you could. Then let them go, knowing that your energy in doing so does not take anything away from you, nor does a demonstration of lack give them more of a push to get where they are going. The energy you channel in order to bless them on their way is from the Divine, who has an inexhaustible supply for everyone. Be peaceful and know it's OK to hang on to your chocolates and jobs.

Self-Punishment Is Not a Means to Deal with Loss

Finding meaning in death is perhaps one of the most difficult aspects of life's adversity. Some may say making spiritual deals helps people to assimilate loss and deal emotionally with devastating circumstances. We want to assume responsibility for our loved ones' chosen state of health or the way they leave the planet. It makes us feel as if we had some control over part of the process or participated in the outcome. But making peace, and thereby coming to terms with loss, has to do partially with accepting that we chart our own soul journeys and departure dates long before we get here, in order to fulfill a purpose. It's a stretch to think that we grasp the intricacies of someone's soul chart and know another's earth-path. Still, departures are great lessons for ourselves, and for those around us.

Making deals is also based upon the expectation of more loss. You are creating a space to invite more of what you don't want. The only space you should be making is a bigger room for more love. Replace self-punishment with a greater capacity to love. Recognize that you have already got additional strength that facilitates your growth. Inspire others to do the same.

If you give your power away instead, you are limiting your own experience of life by giving away your opportunity to question and learn from future circumstances. Not only is it a form of self-punishment but, at a deep level, you are holding on to the belief that you are responsible for someone else's journey, which includes situations they have chosen in order to experience life a certain way. Some choose more difficult conditions than others, for the purpose of evolving their soul. But each of us is responsible for our own chart, and, in the form of families, spouses, parents, communities, and nations, we are all helping one another evolve, or perfect our souls individually and as a group.

The universe does not want you to give up what you enjoy in order that someone else can achieve more, die quicker, or have a better life. The universe wants you to grow, learn, love one another, and make a positive contribution to someone else's soul journey. That is why you signed on for this tour. Life is not a series of punishments, nor do we have to keep on punishing ourselves in order to survive difficult circumstances. We invent that way of thinking all on our own, and we see it reflected in many people we encounter.

How many of you have heard a martyred person say, "God isn't through with me yet!" I have actually seen this aphorism on wall plaques in gift catalogs. How is that an inspiring mantra for living life? Take those plaques, and your faulty thinking, and toss them in Tuesday's garbage pickup. Life is an abundant expression of the universal life force combined with your own special rendition of that force, and the more you put out, the more you will receive.

Inhale Faith Regularly, in Deep Gulps

As a social scientist, I have been trained to find comfort in numbers, although I am equally reliant upon faith. In research, if we set a certain standard and can measure whether an idea or a result exists, then we have a construct for at least a theory. In fact, we might have the basis for a belief.

Just last week, I gained further insight into this concept when I took both my young sons out to dinner at our favorite local sushi restaurant. I was amazed at their worldview, which probably resulted from some schoolwork on world religions. Jason, a critical thinker at thirteen, told me that society feels the need to construct belief systems – and there is not necessarily any proof behind such beliefs. He argued that humans have a natural need to do this in order to explain what cannot be explained. Without proof, he said, why should he subscribe to anything he can't see, especially God?

I was further alarmed when Vaughn, age eleven, chimed in that he's just not sure there is a God, a Goddess, or any higher power, for that matter. I have never forced them to believe anything, because we build beliefs as a result of our own life experiences. Their life experiences will be totally different than mine. Although I can offer a foundation and continually teach them how spirit infiltrates our every move, I can't fill in the blanks for them. That they must do on their own.

> If I didn't have my faith when my dad died . . . I just don't know what I would have done. It's what got me through.
>
> *Sue, wallcovering installer*

I realized the boys were just beginning to question the world at large. They also had a limited view because they had experienced little adversity, failure, loss, or grief in life – some, but not enough to know how important it is to believe there is a reason for it. By the time we reach forty, our adversity résumé is quite long; we've got a vast inventory under our belts in multiple categories. We *need* to believe and depend upon reasons we can't fully explain. Life seems to lead us that way in order to cope.

As we continued to talk about belief systems, I realized that, at their tender ages, they had already been indoctrinated with the sort of comfort that a Cartesian viewpoint provides: if we don't see it, it doesn't exist. How did this happen, I wondered. Do our children have so much difficulty having faith because they see no physical evidence to confirm their parents' belief systems? Or do they simply feel so secure and unblemished by life's circumstances that they feel no need to rely on faith? Faith is different from feedback we receive from our environment. Faith is the underlying assumption for the existence of everything in the entire universe. It is our comfort in knowing it's all there for a reason.

> I've prayed to Mary for so many things in my life – she always seemed to get me results because she's female. I've always felt heard, and that she understood me.
>
> *Connie, pharmacologist, mother of three*

I spent the rest of my wakame salad and miso soup time explaining that not seeing something doesn't mean it's not there. We know love exists, even though we cannot see it. What would the world be like without love? Well then, they replied, let's conduct some focus groups, find out what percentage of people believe in love, and see if it's statistically significant. Their plan for proving the existence of love was to take a poll. We've done a very good job, I thought, of indoctrinating our kids with an overvalued concept of proof.

Overall, I think we need to balance science and faith, especially when it comes to the subject of the soul's journey. Granted, faith sometimes does not give us the level of certainty we want to accept life's bad circumstances. It'd be awfully nice if we'd get a progress report at the day's end that explained just what the heck was going on. Some days we get an unusually large dose of the nasties. But we determine the progress of our soul journey by our own self-evaluations. Knowing the "why" of life's circumstances can't necessarily be part of the report card, because if we knew everything, the *reason* for everything, there would be no point in the dance. We all agree: there doesn't seem to be any consolation in not knowing. And because I am a researcher, it does go against my nature to come up empty-handed in this category; not knowing, after a really good analysis, just doesn't seem acceptable. We seem to think we missed something along the way or left out part of the equation.

We have a dependence on knowing because we don't always cast our net wide enough about our spiritual development. Perhaps we evolve *into* faith because we can't make meaning without it after enough living has gone by. Proof soothes mainly because most of us are limited to our five senses, which serve as our conceptual parameters. Although some are gifted to extend past those limitations in distant realms, or have had extraordinary psychic experiences that defy current logic, the rest of us need pure faith to keep us on track. Never diminish the value of faith. You'll spend less energy on asking why and surrender to not knowing more readily. Find a way to develop unshakable faith in the Divine – it's a participative partnership based upon trust you'll need.

Persevere When People Put You Down

Often we experience perfection and self-love when we've reached a goal. It's a state of bliss – for a moment. We see the result, feel it, live it, but because we haven't changed ourselves enough to resonate with it, the opportunity quickly slips away. People will say, "Well, it wasn't meant for you to have this house, this relationship, this job. It just wasn't meant to be." Or a variation: "If you couldn't hang on to it, it wasn't meant to be yours anyway. You just weren't ready for it." That one really stings.

I've often thought about those expressions, wondering if, by accepting those terms, I would lead a happier, more surrenderful life. I've decided the contrary. Such comments just motivate me to overcome challenges placed in my path. People who regularly deploy these expressions resign themselves to having seen the mountaintop for a few milliseconds, then don't want to do the work to return. It takes a lot of effort to get back up there, and others want you to remain at base camp. By giving you a glimpse of success, the universe is offering you an opportunity to be better prepared for what you will be doing with your time: to refine your true self, have clarity, emanate light, and raise your energy in a way that resonates with that opportunity so that it *does* stick. Becoming stronger through the adversity you experience on the way up (or down, as the case may be) is also about shedding requests that the Divine provide it all for you. You have to do half the work. How? It's simple – just keep going. You *can* work with life's flow without throwing in the towel. It just depends upon your perspective.

Encourage Yourself – You Know Exactly What You Need

You might think that if you had just a little more encouragement, things would be better. Why don't people encourage you to try harder? Life is full of underachievers who expect others to do no better than themselves. So they don't boost you up because they don't believe you can reach the top. What's more, it takes a lot of personal energy from another individual to convince you that you *can* do something. Pep talks are energy-intensive, and if you are inclined to keep putting yourself down, you make the task even more laborious for the person doing the pepping. Unfortunately, unless they are really dear, beloved people in your life, most people will choose among the following classic statements.

Well, it just wasn't meant to be.

God has a plan for you and it looks like it doesn't include_____
_____.

This is a sign from the universe that you should do something else.

Why don't you just quit and pursue something else?

Your parents or siblings never had that and they did just fine.

You're going for too much. Can't you be satisfied with what you have?

You've tried this already and it's never worked before.

Can't you just take a hint from God?

I know what's best for you and it doesn't include_____
_____.

Hearing these sentiments can alert you that something truly *isn't* right with the approach you are using to get what you want, but it doesn't mean you should accept them and give up. Learn to see the connection between self-doubt and put-downs: people often reflect to you what is in your own heart. Listen to what they say, check whether you are doubting your own ability to succeed, then move on. And remember, perseverance is part of dealing with adversity.

Mel Fisher spent years searching for the *Nuestra Señora de Atocha*, a Spanish galleon sunk in a 1622 hurricane off the coast of south Florida. Each morning, before the diving commenced, Fisher was said to have told his crew, "Today's the day!" It took nearly sixteen years, but he finally found one of the richest treasure finds since the opening of King Tut's tomb. In 1985, Fisher estimated the treasure to be worth $400 million, an absolute fortune. He demonstrated positive thinking, staying in the present moment, and perseverance. Whoever said buried treasure was easy to find?

The ultimate, most magnificent treasure lies deep within ourselves – and all of us overachievers don't want to hear the following news flash: the quest might take sixteen years. Constant positive thinking is a result of complete and continual belief in yourself and what you can do. Positive thinking must be joined by actions. Life constantly changes, so your approach should keep changing as well. You also need to ask for a lot of help – from fellow humans as well as the Divine. And know it's OK to go underwater now and then. We can learn from Mel Fisher: get up each day and swing your legs over the side with the anticipation of a kid who just got her first scuba mask. Life awaits you, and your glorious gifts, despite adversity and loss. Today's the day when those circumstances are present for the benefit of your soul – and they exist for your own perfection, designed by your own hand.

BE A WARRIOR AGAINST NEGATIVITY

The most difficult time to inspire others is when things aren't flowing for you. I visualize holding a spiritual shield, warding off negativity in an adversity fencing match. The front of my shield is emblazoned with "Quitters never win and winners never quit." An old, trite saying, but it became a mantra when I was juggling doctoral work while raising two children and while my husband was in a business taking a turn for the worse. So many of my closest friends offered no encouragement for my academic goal during that period. I desperately needed the support but so few of them could relate. I wasted an enormous amount of energy wishing *someone* would reach out.

I remember tallying the assignments during the first semester and thinking there had been some mistake: seventeen papers had to be written in the first semester, plus coursework, exams, deep study, and research projects. I had a two-hour commute every day. Seventeen papers? Halloween costumes became a thing of the past. Between childrearing and running a home, I didn't sleep for years, and my sense of community with my friends went right out the window. Life seemed to go on around me, but I made a choice to continue. The second master's degree and the PhD took six years – not as long as finding the *Atocha*, but it felt like eternity.

> Nurturing is the single most important thing in the world, especially after 9/11, but unfortunately that was very short-lived.
>
> *Priscilla, business owner*

Truthfully, during those years I collectively received far more discouragement than encouragement for the wide variety of my endeavors, which used to devastate me beyond words. We used to keep the classifieds in business with a revolving door of caregivers. My husband and I recently calculated that we employed twenty-two caregivers in the last fifteen years. That alone will challenge anyone's ability to deal with adversity. In the first three months of my PhD work, we had four different women, each bringing a different brand of neurosis into our home. Fortunately, after the fourth one quit during the last two weeks of that term, my mother moved in with us. She showed up at my door, sternly pointing her finger at me, saying, "You are *not* going to quit!" I believe such times in life are when prayers are answered: help and encouragement appear when we are least likely to expect them, and thankfully we are smart enough to recognize we are being assisted in ways we could not possibly imagine.

Everyone needs support, even the most positive thinkers on the planet. We all like to be on the receiving end, but it's just not feasible. Mostly, you must generate it on your own. I've learned that when someone discourages you, they are giving you a reflection of what is in their mind and heart. People who are discouraged themselves or have been disappointed for one reason or another must spend tremendous effort to give you what they can barely generate for themselves. They don't want to take a few moments to lend you a hand. It's out of their comfort zone to encourage someone who might want more, be bigger, go faster than they do. Some people think that by giving something away, even if it is encouragement, compassion, or taking your kids for a night so you can have ten straight hours of peace and quiet, they will generate far less for themselves. So we must always be ready to rely upon ourselves and our source for positive reinforcement.

AVOID NEGATIVE THINKING TRAPS SET BY OTHERS

Have you ever noticed how infectious negative thinking is? Especially when bad jokes, cynicism over politics, or even gossip about friends gets started, it seems those conversations just keep spiraling down into negativity land, until everyone is brought to the lowest common denominator. People with low self-esteem can unconsciously bring you down in other ways because they are skilled at directing your energy from yourself, channeling it directly to their own energy repository. I call them energy lampreys. Beware!

For example, have you been told that you are responsible for another's happiness? This becomes dangerous, because what we're being asked to do is interfere with another's karmic development. By accepting this type of responsibility, we do not allow that person to grow into their own vision of a full life in the form of happiness, good humor, money, excitement, or a lifestyle. We can certainly help one another demonstrate those ideas. But when you adopt another person's vision of what you *should* be doing for them, you are no longer helping. It is not your responsibility to devote your entire life to making another person happy.

Overall, negative thinkers create adversity in our lives, especially when our reactions include guilty feelings. Here are some familiar negative thinking traps we hear.

If you don't have a smile on your face, I just worry about you all the time.

You're the only one I like to do things with.

My life is completely empty without you.

Your mother can't come to the phone – you made her sick.

You don't do enough for me.

I'd be happy if you would only _____.

If you leave me, I'll be miserable and won't know what to do.

I don't need your greeting cards/gifts/loving presence to make me feel better – I just need a little more help around here from you.

These are from people who feel sorry for themselves. They put themselves down, expecting others to pull them up.

We'll try to look nice when we see you, but we're just not fashionable any more.

It's no fun to be old/young/sick/tired/left out.

I never get any breaks.

I'll never live to see my grandchildren.

I've been unhealthy my whole life. Why would I think that's going to change?

I don't deserve_____[a gift you just sent].

I'm never going to get married or have children – I'm too _____

_____.

I am not loved by anyone.

Everything I touch turns bad.

That's easy for you to say, you have the perfect life.

I'm not smart enough/good enough/slim enough/rich enough so I can't_____.

There's no turkey in the oven and I'm eating canned soup because you're not here for the holiday.

You know old people like me. One day they're fine, the next day they're ready to die.

To work against negativity, start with some simple exercises.

EXERCISE: WATER OFF A DUCK'S BACK

Imagine that when you hear these types of comments from people, you can increase your resiliency. Resiliency is about knowing when to listen and when to use your tune-out button. To tune out negative commentary, first imagine you are protected by a light force, letting only the good come through. You are acquiring inner strength greater than what you currently have. You are developing resiliency that will come in handy during another phase in your life.

When you tune out negative commentary that hits your hot buttons, imagine the words sliding off you like water off a duck's back. The negativity floats away from you in an ever moving current of cool water. Think of the people who regularly surround you with negative commentary. Each time you hear a comment that hits your button, summon up your visualization of water off a duck's back. There's no science to it – just imagine negativity sliding off.

EXERCISE: SNAPPY SPIRITUAL COMEBACKS

Go one step further and make a mental effort to change those comments into positive statements. This takes some discipline! Make a list of frequent statements from guilt-ers, martyrs, and negative thinkers. You can respond silently to yourself or out loud, depending upon your level of courage. Practice! Words heal more than you can possibly imagine, and when you learn to express your highest vision of yourself and others, miracles happen.

My life is completely empty without you.
No, it's not, you have the power of divine love in your life.

I never get any breaks.
Yes, you do, you have me for a friend/daughter/son/spouse and I am wonderful.

I am not loved by anyone.
Yes, you are, you are loved unconditionally by your source, whose love for you is endless.

Everything I touch turns bad. (chronic)
Go to a hospital and offer comfort to another. Your beautiful words and touch can help anyone.

Everything I touch turns bad. (just down on life, kids, and kitchen remodeling)
You are so talented. It's not part of my thought process to imagine you as anything less than the beautiful soul I already know you are.

That's easy for you to say, you have the perfect life. (This is good bait because misery loves company – you will exhaust your energy supply by offering anything less than the highest vision of you.)

My life is perfect because my soul is an example of divine perfection in my own individual way. All I am doing is demonstrating the essence of the Divine.

Practice mentally and then begin to deploy your snappy spiritual comebacks. You can combine them with your duck's-back visualization. You will be amazed at how soon you will start to feel like a warrior against negativity!

BE COMFORTED: STARTING OVER IS AN ONGOING JOB

How often have you sent out a proposal, done something for another person, been through a terrible relationship, and proclaimed, "Oh, that's the absolute *last* time. I will *never* go through that again." You may see those same challenges cropping up over and over, especially if you have not changed old patterns of thinking. The way you navigate through those challenges, still keeping your resiliency factor high, is enhanced by self-love. If you don't see the results you want in your life, then start again the next day. Ask for help and be proud of your effort. Starting over just gives you a chance to do it better.

We're always starting over, in one form or another, trying something different: a new job, new relationship, new formula for success, new idea to launch into the world, new philosophy to keep our children on a good track. Subconsciously, we are hitting the refresh button on our screen every day – several times a day, if you really think about it. Learning to be resilient is about refreshing your outlook, staying in present-moment awareness while learning to balance complexity *and* embracing life's contrasts – with open arms, in all the glorious aspects of life. It's a tall order but nobody said it would be easy. You've signed on for the big roller-coaster ride. There is no light without darkness – it's a package deal!

The human condition is rarely free of grief, loss, death, failure, divorce, ill health, difficult relationships, and all sorts of adversity. But our resiliency can be strengthened by knowing that each day begins anew, opening space for positive change. You'll notice that even though your perception of some people or relationships changes, others will tell you that those people are the same as they were before. We simply evolve in our ability to handle them better.

Pain Leads to Peace When We Are Fully Conscious

When we experience loss, in the form of another person leaving, it is absolutely necessary to move through the pain, experience it, grieve, get angry, perhaps resign yourself, in order to move forward. But pain places you in a position to accept comfort – allowing someone else a chance to do *their* soul work. Pain does lead to peace if we put moving forward at the top of the agenda. Moving forward through loss and grief is a lesson in using empty space for love, not for more loss. Find the strength to crack open that space inside you, no matter how painful. Continue exchanging with others and fight the urge to isolate yourself. You will be amazed at what resides within.

> Connecting with someone at a deep level and being there to help them through is amazing, because when you are there for other people, you give so much more of yourself.
>
> *Lisa, charity director*

Many times our own need for comfort is overlooked. Being isolated during periods when we need comfort more than ever

– and not necessarily by choice – is difficult to accept. When my father-in-law died unexpectedly a few years ago, I experienced my own grief as well as empathically experiencing the grief of family and friends. I expected to have my own grief recognized – after all, isn't that a part of the grieving and healing process? However, during the funeral activities and the many encounters I had with clergy and members of the community afterward, the offer of compassion was directed only toward my husband. Over the course of months, I stood beside my husband, whose hand was grasped, his grief acknowledged, while I stood there unrecognized. I wondered, "Are my own feelings of loss not appropriate? Or is my function here to just keep facilitating the process for everyone else while my own grief would be more of a burden on those around me?"

This added even more hurtful heaviness to my plate, but in the end I became stronger and more perceptive. I had to learn how to ask for what I needed; I realized I wasn't going to get it unless I asked. When a close friend was killed in a car accident the following spring, I readily asked for comfort while giving it at the same time. Providing loving support to her grieving family, and my own, seemed easier while I allowed my own grief to run its course. I healed, and healed others, while I grieved. I fully participated in the process of grieving while comforting others. I imposed no limitations for healing, from myself or from others, because I learned how to accept and give simultaneously. I was an open channel for grief – accepting and giving comfort all at once.

I learned my grief lessons well that year, considering that I attended funerals for four other people and gave emotional support to many others whose loved ones had crossed over. It was a far cry from what I had ever experienced previously. The universe does have a way of driving a point home. Comfort equals both input and output, sometimes in a synchronized process leading to healing. Don't be afraid. Use these lessons well when it is your time. It expands your heart and puts you in touch with the whole of humanity.

Sometimes it is difficult to offer the highest vision of ourselves in the form of comfort, because some people are fearful of sharing loss. I suppose as we get older, we just get better at consoling others. But don't ever distance yourself from those who are experiencing adversity. Reaching out is part of your soul story too. Offer everyone comfort, in the best way you know how, for all types of adverse circumstances. Keep calling, send notes, bring dinner, give more hugs. Your resiliency will become astounding. And when you are told, "Things will never be all right again," by those you've assured that it *will* be all right, you've still done a good job. You've just grown your heart tenfold.

Affirm the Positive, Present-Moment Benefits

Accepting life's contrasts at a deep spiritual level means that both good *and* bad serve to define you in your soul journey. We are meant to learn resiliency – we teach our children that from day one. Pick yourself up, keep moving forward, and ask for divine assistance. You will be amazed at how help arrives. Be open to receiving your good, and don't specify the exact means: the universe is infinitely creative and will send it to you in ways you may not even have imagined. Arise each day in a state of thankfulness for what you are learning. Illuminate others with your loving compassion and resolve. You are, without even realizing it, raising the consciousness of everyone around you by your inspiring example. That is why we affirm: *Change is good. I am becoming more resilient with every circumstance. I never give up. Life is a cycle. There's always room for more love. I believe I am evolving every day.*

EXERCISE: WRITE YOUR OWN RESILIENCY AFFIRMATION

Start by writing a description of a circumstance that has been difficult to move through. Remember, you are *going through it*, not stuck there permanently.

Adversity

_____

_____

_____

_____

_____

_____

_____

_____

Now you will write your own affirmation to turn your heartache into victory and joy. But first, remind yourself of what you have learned:

Change is good because I am learning how to_____

_____.

Change in my life is positive because _____

_____.

With each circumstance, I am becoming more resilient
because _____.

I never give up. The world needs my special capabilities of ____

_____.

This change allows me to _____

_____.

The world is a better place with my loving energy intact. My
love changes the world because _____

_____.

This experience reminds me that life is a cycle. My loss provides more room in my life to love _____
_____.

I believe every day I am evolving because _____
_____.

Remember, you are moving through it with ease! Be comforted knowing we are all in it together. Pass Go, collect what you need from the infinite bank of wisdom, and believe you are capable of more than you thought possible.

Adversity Affirmation

_____
_____
_____
_____
_____

Consciously Create Your Day

Here are a few affirmations I have found helpful in navigating through adversity. Use them to help design your own. Remember, each day is a new opportunity to make positive change in your world.

CHANGING JOBS

Today I commit to a new path. I am filled with excitement and anticipation of a new adventure. Those in my immediate future are already welcoming me as a positive addition to their team. Divine guidance has found the best situation for me so that my light can shine brightly.

GRIEF FROM LOSS

*My heartache fills my entire body today, but I know the love
I have for this person who has crossed over is far greater than
my heartache. From this day forward, each time I feel my heart
ache from the absence of this person, I will focus on the love they
brought into my life. I am so very thankful to have been blessed
by their presence. No one is ever lost or gone forever, because love
lasts forever. Every time I feel a heartache coming on, I send out
a greater amount of love to the outer reaches of the universe and
beyond. I am comfortable knowing this person will receive my
love, every day and through every loving thought.*

FACING DIVORCE

*I leave this relationship with grace and dignity. I know my own
soul must grow in an area outside the perimeter of this relationship. No matter how painful the past, I am thankful that this
venture has been part of my learning journey because it helps
me to further define myself. My ability to give and receive love
remains intact. My heart is healing. I have tremendous capacity
to love others, no matter what the circumstances.*

ADDICTION

*I no longer run from life. I now fully engage in what life has to
offer. I rise above any physical need that does not contribute to
my overall health and well-being. I do not need any substance to
hide from life because I love what I have to offer. I am the parent
and my body is the child. I take care of my child-body with love
because I love my beautiful self.*

For more affirmations, see my companion book, *The Women's Book of Empowerment: 323 Affirmations That Change Everyday Problems into Moments of Potential* (The Goddess Network Press, 2005). Available through any major online
book retailer or at www.thegoddessnetwork.net.

Taking Spiritual Inventory:
Design Resiliency into Your Life

Analyze

Take inventory of life's contrasts. List some of your most painful experiences, and how they have allowed you to become stronger. What was the impact on your spiritual development and that of others?

Pain: How I Became Stronger	Self-Learning: What I Taught Myself and Others
_____	_____
_____	_____
_____	_____
_____	_____
_____	_____
_____	_____
_____	_____
_____	_____
_____	_____
_____	_____
_____	_____
_____	_____
_____	_____
_____	_____
_____	_____
_____	_____
_____	_____
_____	_____

Ask yourself:

* Have I been able to release those experiences and view them as positive learning opportunities for myself? For my family? My community?
* What value did I take away from those experiences? Do I keep repeating the same stories? If so, what patterns do I detect?
* Have I been able to move on the upward spiral of spiritual development without bitterness? What benefits are there for me and for others when I see the big picture?
* Is it possible to live life without conflict? Death? Difficult relationships?
* Do I truly believe that painful circumstances in my life have a purpose? Is it true that suffering brings the point home, when it comes to life's lessons?

Affirm

View the big picture. Let's look at life as a soul story. What do you think you are here to learn? Consider patterns in relationships, your challenges, and hardships you have experienced. Write an affirmation that helps you overcome pain or despair. Remember to affirm the good in life!

Walk the Talk

List the realistic actions you will take to heal. How will you act?

_____

_____

_____

_____

_____

_____

_____

_____

_____

_____

_____

Share the Spirit

Share your strengths and weaknesses with your group. What strategies have you found helpful to survive difficult circumstances? Discuss strategies you believe will keep you moving forward without bitterness and self-pity. Consider the following topics for discussion.

* ❀ When others give comfort to you, do you feel that "everything will never be all right" again? Have you already made up your mind that life is beyond your control? Do you believe part of your soul story has included difficult circumstances? If so, what has been the benefit of adversity in your life?
* ❀ Do you wear your difficult circumstances on your sleeve like a badge of honor? Do you feel your past circumstances distinguish you in some way or validate you?
* ❀ Do you believe there is a connection between your difficult circumstances and what you are here to learn in this lifetime? Why or why not? Why do some people seem to have "easy lives"

without strife or complex circumstances? Should we be the judge of other people's lives?

* If we have a loving image of the Divine, why would some people receive a bitter or punishing life while others do not? Does your wisdom tradition have rules or ideas about who issues difficult circumstances and pain in life? If you think you do not choose your own circumstances at the level of the soul, then who does? What does your answer say about who takes the responsibility in your life? Who creates your happiness? Your opportunities?

I SHED MY SHADOW SIDE
IN ORDER TO DISCOVER
MY AUTHENTIC SELF.

Your Authentic Self

Define Who You Are by
Knowing Your True Self

WHO ARE YOU?

Spirituality is my own unique definition. It's what I say, with whom,
how, and where. I'm constantly adding to it as my life changes.

– Pauline, marketing manager

Throughout history, every culture has questioned the nature of
the eternal self and the soul. We've kept a dialogue running from
one generation to the next, handing off our best scientific observations, psychology, and religious convictions about who we are
and how we fit into a vast plan, a plan that gives us assurance that
we are more than what we see in the mirror. It doesn't matter if we
reach consensus or not. As long as we are judgment-free, everyone's ideas have merit. It's designed to be an exploration process.

Religious diversity gives us an opportunity to reach across conceptual miles and discover common ground in our imagery and
saviors, inviting us to open our hearts and embrace similar ideas.
It's an ongoing process of self-definition enhanced by the flavor of
whichever scholarly thought you subscribe to. To date, membership in an exclusive club is not required – no one has cornered the
market on knowing the Divine.

Looking at where we've been and where we're going is all part
of the program, courtesy of our wisdom wrinkles and the inevitable stumbling blocks encountered on the path through kids,
careers, divorces, moving, and aging. Shouldn't life begin to make
sense by the time we're forty and be the expansive experience full
of self-love, self-worth, and self-approval we've heard about in
yoga class? We're supposed to be self-aware by then, pretty much
finished with self-improvement; we've read every self-help book on

the market and, with a bit of luck, should be just plain happy with ourselves.

My dear friend Sue, in a conversation we had about what men want from women they've been married to for twenty years or more, once said, "They just want more of what you've got!" "What's that?" I wondered, as I considered my expanding waistline after the meal we had vigorously attacked after a hike in the northern Michigan woods. "When you get older," she explained, "we simply become more of who we are." Our men want more of the *essence* of us? Insightful words when applied to the journey we take to find ourselves.

It's true: the older we get, the easier it is to settle into an unhindered "who we are" comfort zone, unafraid to express our opinions. We quit worrying over who buys our paintings or whether we show up wearing the proper attire, taking controversy on the chin like WWF wrestlers, knowledge and ego intact. But with wisdom and age comes the profound realization that the more knowledge we acquire, the more we think we know, until we discover we have just had a glimpse of what we *don't* know. On second thought, we realize we cannot possibly achieve a state of knowingness through knowledge itself. At that moment, we resign from structure and intellect and take up residence with the embodiment of intellect, which is none other than our *self*, within this whirlwind we call life, in all its mystery.

That realization makes us ready to dial our own number, 1-800-Spiritual Journey, and prepare for a direct connection to the Divine. But before we begin calling, we must first delve deeply inward and embrace ourselves in the process. We want to have a barrier-free, passionate exchange with our soul, in an effort to permanently define ourselves and the spirit that propels us to greatness.

If you take a stroll through the self-help and spiritual sections of any bookstore, you'll notice a rich spiritual dialogue that runs all over the map. But these works have enough in common that they locate many of our observations on the same route, combining our own beliefs with a truth that is collected from life's experiences and insight. It appears everyone is still asking the same questions about spirituality. What is it? Spirituality is simply the demonstration of the Divine, the life-giving force, the All that constitutes you through every action and thought. It is your realized nature in the form of the highest ideas you can imagine, like trust, courage, wisdom, forgiveness, non-judgment, compassion, pure light, and love, conveyed through every pore of your skin.

Practicing spirituality in today's world will be subject to your own interpretation, as exemplified by many who have previously walked this planet and left distinctive legacies. Yours will also have its own special character, resonating with those who have inspired you, and it may be different than the mainstream or even indefinable. There is no greater freedom than exploring and creating a personal truth that leads you to accept the Divine on your own terms.

> I'm pretty solid in my faith, but as I get older, I'm more comfortable reading outside my religion. There are so many ways to see God.
>
> *Juanita, special events coordinator*

Nothing can prevent you from being spiritual if you allow the true self to emanate, unobstructed by circumstance, and arrive at a place where you are willing to relinquish certainty.

How do you begin finding that place? Take the course everyone on earth has registered for: Spiritual 101. Substitute the poetic for analysis and listen to the beat of your own heart. Then observe the everyday. There's plenty of opportunity to be spiritual, as we've already got the important software downloaded. Installing a new version might get our drivers to recognize some important features, but it's not necessary for our system to work. We come as a complete package.

The true nature, or true self, has always been naked within us in its perfect design. It is our *spirit song*. We are all going to sing differently. Thank goodness we have our own instruments, or life would be mighty boring, but the song operates *through* us. It's interactive and tactile, and in the earth world, it comes from the heart as an indi-

> A good massage and a pedicure give me time to get centered.
>
> *Kari, CEO*

vidualized rendition. To express the true self, internalize the concept of who you are and allow it to become part of your fabric of being. Through emotions, we're going to live the idea and wear it well. It's a *living* idea.

Not long ago, we hosted a graduation party for our two sons. As an afterthought in the party planning, I added a karaoke machine, thinking the kids would enjoy blasting away throughout the evening. To my surprise, the adults assumed complete control over the microphone, especially the mothers, who hilariously navigated through the Seventies, helped somewhat by generous quantities of wine. As I sat and laughed through my friends' attempts at funk, I also noticed the looks on their faces, as each one quit caring about what she sounded like. They sang with gusto and honesty, and overall, their expressions revealed far greater significance than Saturday-night courage: they showed abandoned joy made possible by the largely interpretive exercise of declaring *self*.

After we've stripped away the worry over whether we're going to sound like Celine Dion, self-expression propels us to self-actualization – even if it's in somebody's backyard. We can sing the same song with joy and feel irreplaceable. Who cares if we're a little off key? Jimmy Buffett and Sister Sledge never sounded better.

As I sat there, it occurred to me that most of us spend a lot of time figuring out how to show the world our own rendition of self. It's an innate desire and we just want a captive audience. We want our own music to be acutely *heard*. It's what makes us feel powerful. The problem is that because we're not appearing on the *Today Show*, we dismiss the possibility that we already make a difference.

For most of us, everyday simple acts are opportunities to demonstrate what already exists within: our true self, our song, the same eternal spirit that infiltrates the core of our being. We have permission to sing at work, within our families, in our communities. And in doing so, we discover primary true power, which is the Divine in us, our symphony. We then become *empowered*.

Empowerment is about self power achieved through knowing the true self, not about winning, joining a protest march, or converting an entire populace to your point of view. It's time to revisit our music and put the bras back on, or off, depending upon your cause. Life is about playing your spirit song over and over again in the venue of your own choice.

Why is knowing the source of our own power critical to maintaining a positive outlook on life? Because we are constantly encountering people who attempt to take our power away and diminish our light. Spiritual power is about demonstrating the empowered state *consciously* and artfully, with love, through your actions and with a deep connection to the present. It is a creative exercise, because you have a choice in how to become living art. You *can* bring spirit through yourself – that is how you express your individuality, painting a true self-portrait in the process. Over time, it will become a quilt of your own mythology, sewn in intricate symbolism and meaning, honoring your inner journey and God. When self-awareness of spirit occurs, the art then becomes you. You have realized your *true self* power. And that is why having a firm, unshakable centeredness in who you are will allow you to overcome any adversity placed in your path.

BODY, SOUL, AND SPIRIT

When we identify with the elements of our spirituality, we can understand our purpose. We are composed of body, soul, and spirit. Our physical body, or *physis*, is our flesh-and-blood physical body, or our outer self. It's what we see in the mirror, a vehicle for movement that houses the soul, or the psyche. *Psyche* is a Greek word meaning "soul." Think of your soul, or your inner self, as a unique thumbprint of divine expression. At the core of your identity is spirit. The ancients called it *pneuma/nous*, or spirit/intellect. Intellect does not refer to the mind or what emanates from the mind in the form of thought. It refers to the witness of experience – spirit witnessing life through us. The mystic philosopher Plotinus described the *nous* as the "knowing principle," or what we have inside us that "knows." It is the glue, our center, the subject of every experience. It is our "sense" of being, and our common essential identity.

The Gnostics referred to the *pneuma/nous* as consciousness. Consciousness is the *state* of who we are – knowing who we are while being in the body. It means we are capable of having an awareness of spirit that extends beyond our physical reality, hopefully, more often than not. So, by the Gnostic definition, we don't have a physical body that is sometimes conscious; we are consciousness that is sometimes aware of having a physical body. Our true identity, or our true self, is spirit, or consciousness, which witnesses what our soul experiences.

Knowing the true self means basking in the realization that we are capable of being one with consciousness. It is about coming into being, or *becoming*, within the dynamic experience we call life. We don't realize our true self, or experience spirit, by sitting on the couch and watching what the world is up to on network television. We bring spirit through us by experiencing life through the soul and the body. If you accept this translation, it means that your origin stems from being spirit, and that the gift of life, or your soul journey, is to allow it to live through you. You are inviting spirit, or your true self, to express its *self*. In that way, you become conscious of spirit through the choices you make.

You begin to enter a state of alignment with spirit. You are working toward *being*.

What is the single most difficult challenge in facing your adversity? It is to remember that every person is an individual spark of spirit, or the Divine. When you focus on being spirit more often, and see others the same way, and when your body and soul are aligned with spirit, you grow into a living expression of the Divine within you (the inward) and of the All (the outward), because you are constantly transforming the world in the process.

The new age balancing act is not juggling kids and a career. It is learning how to be in tune with spirit, which is the equilibrium we strike between being and becoming, while genuinely loving the true self. We must love our constitutional essence – fiercely love ourselves as we love the Divine, because they are one and the same. We're always becoming, which is why the body and the soul are in a constant state of flux, even changing outfits over many lifetimes, but the spirit is constant. The spirit already knows how to be. Our job is to find the balance between being and becoming.

The soul and the body are not only what becomes conscious over time. We are also a totality, composed of consciousness, demonstrating spirit *through* a body and soul; hence the expression "As within, so without." It means that what we create in our experiences reflects what is inside us, which is a dynamic composite of our intellect and our emotion. It occurs in our individual life, but it is also a sum total of everyone on earth. Our goal is to become a conscious expression of spirit during our soul's unique learning agenda and get everyone on the same page of consciousness evolution. Hopefully, we can get being and becoming straight before we depart the planet.

What is the relationship between the body, the soul, and the spirit? Plotinus thought the psyche (soul) was not in the body, but the body was in the psyche. What he meant was that we steer the body, like a car, and the soul does the steering. Although consciousness is our fuel and our reason for driving the car, we also participate in the drive. Our soul decides where it wants to go and the body follows along for the ride. The body has also been thought to be an expression of the soul, which is what many body-soul-spirit practitioners have successfully taught. Louise Hay taught millions of people how to diagnose disease and physical ailments by understanding the body's deeper expression, encouraging people to first heal dis-ease within. From this point of view, what is imbalanced in the body, as an outward expression of what is within, is not determined solely by physical diagnosis. It is about what is lacking, or imbalanced, in the soul, which seems to have its own rhythm. Therefore, our physical ailments are part of the curriculum because we bring certain limitations in our lives, or challenges that help to focus our self-development on certain life themes.

No matter what wisdom tradition you explore to widen your field of vision, the relationship of body, soul, and spirit may very well be debated into infinity. What's the most basic message for everyday living? By embracing who we are from within, and projecting the idea outward, we experience a flow of a certain kind of awareness. And here's the most liberating part: we are all one in consciousness, or a state of shared awareness. Although we are experiencing life *through* the body and soul, spirit remains constant. The consensus on the subject is overwhelming: spirit is one, it is the All, and we are certainly in the All. Although what is reflected in the mirror is different for everyone, we've got the same soul substance, permanently connected to spirit/consciousness.

WHAT'S CONSCIOUSNESS?

Consciousness is like light. If we take light into a completely dark room, its energy illuminates objects in a room. These objects reflect the light, giving us the ability to see them, so we can view the furniture, windows, and rugs. We have a sensory experience; thoughts and feelings arise as a result of what we see. Did we like the colors? Was the space pleasing to us? Could we improve the room? But without light there is nothing to reflect. It's the objects that make the light exist. Consciousness is like the light because it is defined *by* the objects that reflect it.

Without light, what is left is nothingness, the unknown. There is nothing to define and no definer. There's no dimension and we're not aware of any experience. The dark room represents the unconscious state, or an emptiness of the conscious state. Consciousness is *that* which *is*, and unconsciousness is *that* which is *not*. The unconscious does not bear witness to any experience. It has no name, it is indefinable, ineffable. It is only the void. The unconscious state, or what is *not*, is called a mystery because it has no dimension. But the *absence* of consciousness (no light) and what we see and experience in the room (our bodies, our senses, the furniture) are both included in the totality of the universe. The unconscious cannot be described because it has no characteristics. In short, we are what is and what is not, which is the All.

> The more I explore my own spiritual practice, the closer I feel to spirit. I need my own rules.
>
> *Roberta, doctoral student*

In non-metaphoric terms, what illuminates consciousness, or gives it experience, so it can define itself? You do, through your individual stories, your triumphs and travels. We are an entire collection of souls, each of whom brings a unique angle to the whole process. Having a soul and a body helps define consciousness in ongoing and diverse patterns. It's the most basic soul work we all do, which is astonishing. Next time someone asks you what you do for a living, tell them you are helping to define consciousness by experiencing your point of view. Without you, the system can't work. You are a co-creator with spirit. Feel delight, and know you are free no matter what your situation. Live with the potential for ultimate joy as you define consciousness and permit it to unfold in your life.

HOW WE BLOCK OUR MUSIC

I think we get into trouble when we narrow our lens and allow our spirituality to become a dogmatic concern, overcomplicated by rules. Our spiritual status, and consequently the positive image of our selves, has unfortunately been skewered by fear: of the opposite gender, sin, color, alternative philosophies, death, the unknown, different cultures, sex, making mistakes, those who we imagine have power over us. Fear enables us to hold our selves back. It negates the spirit within us, which we *do* have choice in expressing.

Lately our society, in the spirit of mutual respect, free speech, and religious tolerance, has adopted a "hands-off" posture toward spirituality. In order to work together and attend school, we've decided we can't talk about spirit, our source, our reason for being here, or our "beingness" because we can't agree on the interpretation. Fair enough – we can't all have the same image of the Divine. How man and woman came to be is a touchy subject. Thus we've detached and formed an illusion of separateness that has stripped away all identities of who we are at a primary spiritual level.

We're told in grade school that all men (note to founding parents – add "and women") are created equal, that they are endowed by their creator. We acknowledge that we have a spirit somewhere in our purview, but it's been compartmentalized. We think we can be happy without knowing the true self, and nothing could be further from the truth we hold self-evident: we have been *gifted* by our creator. Our reason for being here is to *be* – we are part of a universal whole that is evident through our individual, innate gifts. We can't feel good (God) and achieve our dreams without the entire ensemble, all the way down to the foundation garments.

For the package to work, and so far it does, the All or the source – spirit, God, consciousness, unconsciousness – must always change because what we are thinking and feeling is always changing. Do not forget: everyone creates together in a participative endeavor. That is why you are so important. You are constantly contributing to an enormous composite of the totality of the universe! That alone is a powerful feeling: your presence, within a dynamic system of organized complexity, helps to define All that *is* (and is *not*, if you really want a broad outlook). You belong. You contribute. Your valuable journey is your input to a divine database. You have a say in deciding how and what we all become through your conscious awareness.

LOSING YOUR MASK AND DISCOVERING YOUR SELF

The All, the self, and the unconscious are certainly not new ideas, especially in the field of spiritual psychology. Carl Jung, the founder of analytical psychology, thought the deepest part of the mind extended far beyond the parameters of an individual. He called it the "collective unconscious" and viewed it as a possession of all humanity, readily accessible through archetypes that shape the development of our lives by showing us a universal pattern of human behavior we adopt in life. Identifying with a particular archetype – for example, a mythological character such as Odysseus, the seeker, or Artemis, the independent and competitive goddess – can help us make sense of our own beliefs or actions. When we embody those qualities, like building from a construction blueprint, we identify with who we are. We make sense of our pattern and "become" the house.

Jung envisioned the self as the central organizing archetype in the human psyche, the center of the unconscious. As we engage in an effort to define self (the process of individuation), we bring together all the qualities we develop as individuals, both conscious and unconscious. The first part of the process involves the symbiosis of the healthy persona, or mask, that we adopt in the first half of life, in order to cope with the demands of society, with the discovery of comprehensive meaning and wholeness in the second half of life. Essentially, we complement our strengths with their forgotten opposites, as we reconcile our persona, or outside presentation, and tell the ego to take a back seat in organizing what we show the world.

> In the old days, I cared so much about my clothes, the house, where I traveled. Now it's beginning not to matter because I'm thinking about inner peace more often.
>
> *Ann, age fifty, business owner and mother*

Middle-agers take note: before you knock yourself unconscious and tell your ego to lighten up, realize that coming to full circle in the second part of life mirrors your innate desire to explore the relationship between the inner and outer worlds. We want to reconcile what we've done with our *selves*. It takes us half our life to remember what we have forgotten, because we are coping with the everyday. And after that, we realize that self-discovery is not the only goal. It only prepares us for yet another phase: the need to demonstrate who we are.

In order to discover your authentic self in a process to become "whole," there is no choice but to cast off Jung's mask and take a peek at your shadow side. What has laid stagnant for too long; which ideas no longer serve you about who you are? Do you feel that your inner world defines your outer world? All we see in the outer world is an expression of our inner selves. You are a Leonardo da Vinci of the creative force of All that exists, and you honor it by being your true *self*. In an abstract sense, it is an awakening to your own divinity. According to Shakespeare, we can choose to be or not to be every day, by opening our rational minds to the possibility that we *are* divine from the minute we come on the scene – we're just creating additional content. Everyone has the capability of being who they are. Be all you can be, which is nothing less than your true self.

If you make a direct call to the Divine, you will know you are both self and source. You are in the same area code. The only difference between you and the totality of the Divine is that you do not have perfect awareness of All that is, a perfect memory of everything that has transpired since the beginning, and perfect preservation of love. You haven't given perfect guidance to everyone involved. Sure, it's something we can work toward, but even so, at this moment in time, the whole and the part are present within each other – we're just the center of choice, helping to define the All. Be delighted at knowing you are so important. Let that realization resonate within you, let it rip, let it go, let it flow like a river, let it *be*. It is the first, surest, and most efficient beginning to find your self. Remember, the path to self begins inside. Look in a mirror and love your self. You are absolutely divine.

The Authentic Self Versus the Socially Constructed Self

There is a big difference between the authentic self and the socially constructed self, or the personality. Defining our selves by what we see does help to form our personality and is a consequence of living in a physical world. Our self-opinion, self-image, and self-confidence are partially shaped by other people. We've all taken personality tests, or analyzed our personalities, and selected friends on the basis of their personalities. From the minute we come home from the hospital, our personalities begin to be defined – by our environment, by others of influence, or by our own hand.

However, the personality is not your true self; it is a role we adopt along the way in order to cope. It tends to be fragile and thrives on approval, sometimes seeking to be sustained by power. If we choose to identify our entire being with an outer presentation, we make our biggest mistake. The true source of our power is *not* the ego or the personality, it is our authentic self, our true self, or spirit. When we reach a point in life where we look to spirit or consciousness as our foundation, we know we are not what we see – we are enlightened only when we know we are pure spirit underneath.

That's why dictators and other misguided leaders get themselves into so much trouble; they are operating from the perimeter and not from the true self. They think the source of their power will be enhanced by increasing their own ideas of self–importance, placing their false selves on a pedestal; consequently, they put their divine power in the back row. They are "full of themselves" but not of their expanded selves. They want others to stroke their individual talent or position of power but have forgotten they are simply a frequency that the Divine operates on. They are out of tune, their intentions are wrong, and essentially, by wanting constant reinforcement and making bad choices, they are doing exactly the opposite of what they desire – and that is to enhance their power. They are not operating from the higher self. Power used to glorify the false self always crumbles in the end.

Remember that, when you encounter egotistical people in your own life. Their act of self-love is directed to their ego, and they may think their accoutrements enhance their power. They are not empowered by their true self. True power comes from allowing the Divine to work through you, which is the real meaning of being "self-centered" or "self-aware," which is good. That is what we appreciate and admire in others, and passionately love. Self recognizes self at an unconscious level, like perfect substance reflected in a mirror. When powerful people are focused only on their outer layers, we usually react by being either hypnotized or completely repelled.

Never claim your physical identity as your true self. You are not the body, and even though you have a soul that may help cart you around, you must reach *beyond* your individual soul to realize your true being. Stay focused on consciousness as your essential nature: it is the reason for being, the reason for the reason, the step in your groove. You will be enlightened by knowing who you are: a state of complete light and love, which is spirit.

Two Fundamental Assumptions About the Divine and You

In research, assumptions provide a foundation, or infrastructure, for our conceptual models. As there are many paths to defining a truth, we're not all going to have the same fundamental assumptions underlying our ideas, especially those that help you make the leap in knowing you are divine. In a discussion about spirit, you might rely upon the stories, myths, or teachings offered by many enlightened people in addition to some of your own insight gathered from the experience of living. Here are two common assumptions that help us make sense of who we are.

The Divine is All (everything) and we are part of All that is; therefore, we are never separate from the Divine.
This is the tallest hurdle for most people to overcome: why do we have difficulty seeing ourselves as divine beings? We are part of the Divine and already know what *being* is about. The Divine is All. That means everything that was, is, and is about to be. If the Divine is eternal, that means timeless and without intermission, including the previews as well as the sequel. The Divine cannot be something separate from us,

higher or lower; it infiltrates every aspect of our being, at all times.

For example, if I create a fish, I can say that the fish is an entirely separate product of my thinking, of my "thought skill" as a fish designer. I have produced something of value, it works, it looks great, and I send it off in the ocean on its path to whatever a fish might need to experience. But I, as the fish designer, am not separate from the fish. The fish holds my image of what it is: it has the *idea* of creation, the intellectual blueprint, the *knowing* of what was present in my mind as I created it. Therefore, I am part of the fish, and because it will make other fish and perpetuate itself, evolve, or sustain someone or something, I will *always* be connected to the fish, in the past, present, and future.

I also gave the fish energy to power itself so it can live on its own. I did not create the energy from outside of myself, just pulling it out of thin air. If I am All that is, then the energy came from within me, as some aspect of my being. Therefore, if I give the fish energy to power itself, I am also present within it, because it is part of All that is, which is me.

This first fundamental assumption illustrates that we are more like fish than we think. Put yourself in the position of the Divine for a moment. The Divine is all-encompassing and part of All that exists at any point in time. At this very moment, *you* are part of All that is. Therefore, you are never separate from the Divine.

There is elegance in unity, a simplicity that transcends all religions, races, genders, sciences, and philosophies. If this fundamental assumption underlies your life, you will begin to live knowing it is impossible for you to be anything other than as one with everyone else. You are permanently joined at the hip not only with the Divine but with every person on the planet, past, present, and future. At the fundamental level, there is no separateness.

Because we are part of the Divine, we are the same substance. That means we're divine too. Science gets us thinking about ourselves in a universal perspective, surprisingly, by picking apart our essence through reductionism. What science has uncovered through holograms and their implications for the ideas of part and whole lend further insight as to who we are.

A three-dimensional hologram is created by bouncing a laser beam of light off an object, then bouncing another laser beam off the reflected light of the first. The interference pattern – the area where the two beams come together – is captured on film. When the film is developed, and illuminated by another laser beam, a three-dimensional image of the original object appears. What's remarkable is that if a hologram of a rose is cut in half and then illuminated by a laser beam, each half will still be found to contain the entire image of the rose. If we keep dividing that rose, over and over again, each film would contain an intact, although smaller, version of the rose. Every part of a hologram contains all the information possessed by the whole, implying that the idea of separateness is an illusion.

> I think God is everywhere; we just don't take time to see.
>
> *Georgi, property manager*

It is entirely possible that our souls work the same way. This is not proven yet, but it is certainly possible if we accept what the hologram suggests. There is a deeper level of reality, an underlying unity that explains our physical reality, like the rose. Consult the research on the matter and you'll find it is not such a stretch to rethink our nature. We're like subatomic particles: the distance between them is only an illusion, and our separateness is also illusory because we see only a portion of reality. In the big picture, at the level of consciousness, all is infinitely interconnected. Location doesn't matter, because we are projections of a much deeper order, subject only to our own perceptions of limitation. In a holographic universe, we are in charge of altering our perceptions of reality, without space or time.

It's helpful to look at such phenomena regularly, when searching for understanding of who we are. We've been told that the source is divine. But we've already established that the Divine is all and we are part of the Divine. So does that make us all the same? At an abstract level, why would we be different? By definition, "divine" means of, relating to, or proceeding directly from God. Many wisdom traditions have stressed that we are far less than God; God is perfect, and it appears we are not God because we are certainly not perfect, as our numerous faults have shown over the centuries. But why do we think we aren't perfect in what we are *designed* to be? Or what we are designed to become?

Our purpose seems perfectly logical. If we are engaged in a learning journey for our soul, to perfect the soul, then we are entitled to make a few errors, even though we may have seen a few teachers who have been able to pass the course without doing any homework. It doesn't mean we are *not* divine, not God substance. All is within everything else, as science would have it, and we are the rose replicated. Our spirit contains all the information possessed by the whole. We are, in fact, a smaller whole of the totality of spirit. Our self *is* God, our lives are God, our experiences are part of All that is, was, and ever will be; therefore, we are operating within, in all dimensions, as God, or the Divine.

If we rely upon the universe for inspiration, we already know that subatomic particles, such as electrons, are able to communicate instantly regardless of the distance separating them. Why not take comfort from science and rethink the distance between us and our spirit?

What Does It Mean to Be Divine?

Let's forget about woman power, man power, teen power, military power, and flower power for a moment. We would do well to express divine power more often, by grasping the meaning of the higher self, or the "divine I." Those who explore the Gnostic gospels find lessons that explain why everyone has the power to impart *gnosis*, direct experiential knowledge of God, by realizing that we are more than part of the whole. The Gnostic gospels were among a collection of documents found at Nag Hammadi, an ancient city in upper Egypt. They predate the Bible. Among them is the Gospel of Truth, written by Valentinus, an Alexandrian Gnostic poet in the second century. Valentinus taught that when the human self and the "divine I" are interconnected, they achieve perfection and eternity, two fairly powerful ideas.

The Gnostics were mystic and creative thinkers. They had no knowledge of holograms, but they believed that each person has a mortal lower self called the *eidolon* and an immortal higher self, the *daemon*, considered to be each person's spiritual identity. The eidolon is the physical body, the embodied self, and the ego/personality. The daemon is the true self, the spirit – a portion of the Divine given to each individual, representing *part of the whole*, or a person's spiritual connection to God.

The Gnostics taught that creation goes beyond the physical and the duality of the higher/lower self, the two complementary aspects of our being. They believed in one spirit shared by everyone: a "universal self" which inhabits everyone. Since each soul is part of this "God-soul," when we embrace our selves, or understand our true identity, we know we are also made of divine substance. They lessened the distance between their students and God through the realization that the same consciousness inhabits everyone. And by embracing that consciousness within, they discovered we are one with God and we *are* God. This provides the opportunity to experience a state of enlightenment.

In Western theology, God has been tied up with the dualistic categories of transcendence and immanence. Traditionally, the Divine has been viewed as dominant over nature and human nature, and ascribed *transcendent* qualities, meaning "surpassing" or "supreme." If we can be part of the Divine only by transcending, the goal seems unattainable, at least in this earthly realm, a seedbed of sin where we must deny our human impulses to feel holier, or closer to God. In fact, the concept of rising to meet divinity is about raising our spiritual awareness to meet God in any situation. We are meant to be united with the Divine, because it is our natural state, but unfortunately the idea has been spiked with all sorts of negative messages about aspects of our bodies and denying our sexuality. You still have to take your body and soul along to raise your spiritual awareness, because you are currently *in* a body, and indeed you have embarked on a physical chapter of your soul journey. Love your body as a sacred vessel, and your soul for the opportunity it gives you to learn while you are raising your spiritual awareness.

> When I meditate or pray, I feel spiritual.
>
> *Dorothy, salesperson*

Being divine also reflects *immanent* characteristics, because the Divine permeates all we see, touch, and feel, and we certainly are part of what we observe. "Immanent" means "existing within." It means that God *does* exist within you, within human nature, and in nature itself, which sustains your body and provides you with all the enriching earth experiences that allow you to learn. If spirit permeates everything, then that would mean "as above, so below." It's a bit like having a foothold in two very big, dynamic ideas, both transcendent and immanent. The Divine is everywhere, not just in some unattainable galaxy above or beyond your grasp. But where do we find our selves within this seemingly dual formula?

In Vedantic philosophy, a branch of Hindu mysticism, we discover the Mandukya Upanishads, considered to be the work of Indian sages who lived between 3,000 and 2,500 years ago. They are among the oldest collections of spiritual messages on record, referring to the self as a unitary consciousness. Undifferentiated unity is the self: a single mind, void of all contents, a place where the individual self merges with the universal self, or Brahman. It is a world soul, beyond duality or multiplicity, where the soul realizes its own identity with the Divine. "All this is Brahman; this self is Brahman" means that the self is God.

Found in the Bhagavad Gita, a gospel of Hinduism, is the concept that the Atman, the self, dwells in all beings, but the creative energy of Brahman is that which causes all existences to come into being. In the Upanishads, the concept "Brahman is all and the Atman is Brahman" means that anyone who realizes or becomes *conscious* of the Atman, or the higher self, reaches Brahman, which is the supreme spirit. By having such awareness, we know we are derived from a single source. This idea reminds us that as long as we are conscious of our individual self, we don't have to become the universal self. We always were that self. And in that moment of illumination, we realize our truth once again: that we meet our selves neither on the way up nor on the way down, we simply dissolve into being.

In Hinduism, as in many world religions, the unitive nature of the divine ground, which I interpret as the abstract space where we congregate with God, is achieved through an act of choice. We have the potential, the *choice* to become what we already are. We can be unified with the Divine not in some revelation in an afterlife, but here and *now*. We can demonstrate our divine substance here on earth, in the form of our work, through our relationships, and by loving one another.

So by identifying with God, as the Divine, we discover who we are in our soul studies. Are you ready for your exam question?

Q: Who are we?

A: We are one, we are a unitive, divine substance. Our authentic self is our true self, which is divine.

For 100 points extra credit, if you answer in five sentences or less:

Q: Where do we find the true self?

A: It exists inside of us. We are inherently divine substance by having an awareness of that substance. We are everywhere. We are the total sum of the entire life force, of all energy in existence. And there is no separation at the fundamental level.

TO BE OR NOT TO BE

To be conscious, you must focus on the permanent presence of what constitutes you, the source, who is witnessing your experience. Stop focusing on *what* you experience. When you allow the presence within you to be your witness, you will allow consciousness to flow. You will become conscious of consciousness. It is natural, effortless, and spontaneous to exist in a state of consciousness as long as we know we are witnessing the soul/psyche who appears to be a person. The Gnostics taught that even though we are active participants in the world, we are also a witness to that experience through conscious awareness.

If we radiate from inside as a stream of consciousness, our life experiences bear witness to our soul. At first glance, we appear to one another as separate individuals. Remember, life itself is not the illusion – that is the mistake you will make in thinking that all we've got to do is transcend to a higher realm. Don't forget about the work that needs to be done here and now. The illusion we are born into is that of *separateness*, because we all look different, have different bodies, and have unique personalities. If we go deeper within, beyond the light, back into darkness and even before *appearing*, we would simply "be." We'd find ourselves simply in a state of beingness.

When we choose to identify with a state of beingness, we are choosing to identify with the whole concept of All that is and is not – even what is before consciousness, or without it. When we meditate, pray, or get quiet, and focus our attention within, we can strip away all identities and labels of who we think we are and the roles we play. We can shed images of God that make us feel less than meaningful, images to which we might have assigned far less than ideal human qualities. We leave everything behind and enter an abstract space that everyone exists in, and doesn't exist in, at the same time. We simply know that *we are* – a very good place to be. Where, or what else, could we be? We can't get away from our selves. You'll find "being" on a regular basis allows you to identify with every-one. It is a daily equalizer, helping keep your perspective on living a balanced life because, at a fundamental level, you are always the same as the next person. We're all in it together.

> I attend church to worship with others. I garden to be with God.
>
> *Cybil, community volunteer*

The self articulates by giving us the power to co-create real-ity. Calling ourselves co-creators implies that we are God. It's an outlook than means viewing the world, or your circumstances, as something that can be changed to what you desire. It requires a shift from seeing yourself as separate from spirit – the creative force that is both thought and the power to animate, to manifest thought into form – to *identifying* with that force. It's a more integrated view of who you are and what you can do; it moves you, philosophically, from one who is animated, who is simply moved around by circumstance, into the one who does the animating.

This fundamental change of outlook is the basis of all empow-ered thinking. It explains why we're responsible for what we see in the world. This idea has been a tough sell over the centuries, especially when we observe people getting the short end of the stick, through poverty, illness, catastrophe, or discrimination. It's easier to come up with all sorts of explanations about the state of the world that do not place any responsibility on what we've done. But the world won't change unless we put forth the effort. In every action of our lives, we are co-creating with a shared mind, or one God. It means we *can* speak the same language of spirit by processing the world through our thoughts, emotions, and actions. Every person on earth is on a soul journey to experience life for their own self-development. We manifest, or demonstrate, what we hold in our thoughts; otherwise, the journey makes no sense. We can create poverty and discrimination or choose to do away with them. It's our choice – and not as abstract as it sounds.

Every day and always, you exist and are as important as everyone else. Not easy, when you look at what's on your plate. But if we get in the habit of resetting our thinking while engaged in living life, and become consciousness expressing itself through a series of experiences, we become part of what we are choosing to do and also part of our beingness. We are *achad*, a united one, one power, one presence. And that means we are connected to one another, and to our source, always. There is no other way to be.

Using Affirmations to Find You

Remembering who we are eliminates obstacles to making our own spiritual composition shine in the world, for the benefit of others. Negative circumstances or family relationships often create a barrier between you and your image of your self. Your family was probably not perfect for a reason but, at a soul level, you chose them as a learning environment. They also unconsciously gave you a few roadblocks to make it *necessary* for you to develop into your higher self. If you had it tough, accept it, and quit bashing your head against the wall, wondering why you wound up in a family of aliens. Each day, move forward to increase your energy level and stop blaming others, society, and the world. You'll pick up speed knowing you have selected more difficult circumstances than others in order to evolve more fully, and rapidly, into your self.

Why does knowing who you are make it possible to take ownership of your life? Because you are able to simplify, accept, surrender, and practice compassion and forgiveness more easily. As you think, so shall you be. Clear the spigot of what has held you back in the past; not a single reason exists that will prevent your true self from flowing. Turn on the faucet and affirm that you are a beautiful illustration of perfect light.

Don't ever be afraid to take a look in the mirror. Initially, you may create a definition of you that is based on illusion. You are not your clothes, you are not your wrinkles, and you are certainly not the body. You are not where you live, how much formal education you have, how much money you make, or who you know. Your worth is not determined by possessions or by holding a position of organizational authority. You can't demonstrate a life-giving force in every action and thought if you identify yourself solely by what you see. Finding self is about allowing your essence to express itself at an intuitive level, knowing what you like to do, what you are good at doing, and cultivating those inherent qualities with love. Know where your true power resides and regularly affirm that you are rising above your circumstances.

Many people I meet seem to resonate with a core within them, no matter their situation. They know the difference between doing what they need to do to cope and doing what they want to do to resonate with their own essence. Their essence is a combination of knowing the true source of their own power, and letting that which is within operate as a communications network. They are, both consciously and unconsciously, broadcasting the power within and giving it their own special rendition wherever life has plunked them. We would all do better in life if we held on to this simple image of co-creation of the life force we all share.

So love God, love the Divine, love your consciousness, and love your authentic self. *That is why we affirm*: I am conscious of who I am. I am my true self, I am loved and beloved, and I am in love with my self. I am a marvelous spark of the Divine and celebrate my remarkable learning journey. I am timeless, living without boundary, and full of my beautiful, unique, and divine self.

Consciously Create Your Day

Your life is a demonstration of spirit. You are filled with the Divine. To continue to correct old programming that may hold you back from this knowledge, here are a few affirmations to help you reinforce the Divine within.

Don't Feel Special

I am an important and unique spark of the Divine, just like everyone on the planet! There is but one dimension of love and we all channel from the same source. There is but one universal order, even though we may speak to that voice in different languages. I am challenged to step outside my intellectual boundaries and facilitate a loving acceptance for people in my life, no matter how they label their source. I am a universal human filled with the presence of the Divine wherever I go.

Aging

Each stage in my life is wonderful. My wisdom and experience acquired from life make me a person who has a lot to offer the world. Every moment I continue to engage in the world is valuable to others. I no longer need disease or illness to secure a place in the world. I am shining, with all my wisdom, in my security. I feel safe knowing no one can take my place.

Bad Self-Image

When I look in the mirror, I see a loving person. My capacity to love knows no boundaries. I accept myself and love what I see in the mirror. There are no imperfections because I am perfectly constructed. I am an example of a miracle and a spiritual work in progress.

Unrecognized Talents

I am a unique and beloved individual who has already changed the world by being present. I am filled with joy knowing I have offered the world my gifts. I shine no matter what my family says; my talents reach far outside of this realm. I now focus on what my talents can do for the greater good. I love what I can do!

For more affirmations, see my companion book, *The Women's Book of Empowerment: 323 Affirmations That Change Everyday Problems into Moments of Potential* (The Goddess Network Press, 2005). Available through any major online book retailer or at www.thegoddessnetwork.net.

Taking Spiritual Inventory:
What Constitutes Your Authentic Self?

Analyze

Have you allowed people, jobs, relationships, or circumstances in your life to create a definition of who you are? List your sources of influence, with the most powerful at the top of the list. Ask yourself:

* Has this situation led me to discovering more of who I am?
* Has this person supported me in bringing out my best?
* What has prevented me from expressing my talents? My opinions?
* What is the single most important thing I do that makes me feel I am expressing my true self? Have I spent enough time cultivating my gift to the world? How often do I spend time in my self-expression?
* In my occupation, am I able to allow my true self to operate through me? If so, how?
* As I consider the patterns I have created in my life, what do I think my soul is here to learn? Do these patterns occur repeatedly? What could they mean?
* What events in my life have signaled the need to look deeper within to find meaning?

Affirm

Affirm the existence of your true self by centering your awareness and feeling the source of spiritual power. Ask whether you have allowed anyone, or any circumstance, to take away your power to create the life you want. Do old hurts keep manifesting in your relationships? Affirm to release those feelings and affirm that you are empowered with divine love.

Loving My True Self

*Because I love my self, I release old hurts forever, making it easy
for me to demonstrate the Divine in my every action and thought.
I play an important part in the world's work, which helps to
evolve my soul. I nourish my self when I am in a state of self-love.*

Self Honor

*My soul magnifies the Divine through experience. I am awakening
to my own sense of purpose and to my higher self. I am connected
to my source through my experiences. I honor my soul and the All
by working to expand the idea that spirit is in everything I do.*

Now write your own affirmation that allows you to feel empowered
by spirit.

_____

_____

_____

_____

Walk the Talk

Frustration with life is sometimes a result of expecting too much
after we fill our minds with doing instead of being. What will you
do this week to begin an expanded state of awareness and surrender to your soul journey? List three areas where you can permit life
to happen through you, without fighting upstream.

_____

_____

_____

_____

Share the Spirit

What changes can you make in your life during the next year that
will help you express your true self? List those changes, after shar-

ing your beliefs about your concept of spirit at work in your life. Have those beliefs facilitated your self-expression, or inhibited you? Have you been able to grow with those beliefs intact? Discuss with your group the idea of being one with All that exists. If you accept that idea, how has it changed your life so far? How could it change your life now? If you can't accept the idea, talk about why. Share any experiences in your life that may have brought you to that conclusion.

Or try with your group a meditation called "Spiritual Superhighway." Having a better understanding of our source, or our true self, is often accomplished through meditation: take a moment to connect with your center of wisdom and open your mind to the possibility that we are far more than just physical bodies. Open your mind to becoming one with a higher power with this exercise. You can have someone guide you while in a group by reading out loud the following guided meditation. Visualize the scenario below.

Sit in a comfortable position. Close your eyes and breathe deeply. Imagine you are breathing in a beautiful shade of pink. With every breath you take, the pink stays in your body and fills every part of you, from your fingertips to your toes. When you feel full of the beautiful color, imagine you are on a spiritual superhighway. You are traveling on a bright light path that reaches across the fabric of time and the universe. You are on the path to meet the Divine. As you reach the halfway point, you are embraced and lovingly thanked by God for all you do. Stay in this embrace until you feel completely loved and appreciated for all you are experiencing on earth. Visualize the Divine permeating your entire being, as you become a fusion of your self and the Divine. As you begin to return to the earth plane with the Divine, know that you can travel on this spiritual superhighway at any time you feel lonely. Know that you are loved. Take that feeling with you throughout this day, every day, and always.

I HAVE EVERYTHING I
NEED IN LIFE. MY SUPPLY
IS LIMITLESS AND I
CONTINUALLY ACCEPT
GIFTS FROM THE UNIVERSE.

Abundance

Create a Mental Equivalent
to Manifest What You Desire

Open Up to Abundance

*I see myself in what I create. Whatever
I think, I can make it happen.*

– Kelly, interior designer

Practicing the presence of self is about observing the Divine in
all things and people, despite appearances to the contrary. We are
loved by others when we identify with our true self because spirit
always recognizes spirit – we're the same soul substance. As our
souls evolve during our lifetime, we must find ways to bring our
own gifts to the world. It's a challenge! Although we are spiritual
beings, living in a physical world requires us to find ways to channel our energy in the form of meaningful work. And we feel great
when our work is appreciated and brings abundance as a result.

Through positive, sustained effort, our soul work can become
effortless, an articulation of both our physical and our spiritual
natures, allowing us to feel prosperous and see material results.
It's an exercise in opening our channel to the Divine. Once we are
actively engaged in the process, we can experience a life filled with
abundance. How do we align with our spiritual side and get financial results? If we change our thoughts and attitudes, is it possible
to change our financial condition?

Know You Already Have Everything

Although living the simple life worked for Diogenes – who once
decided to throw away his last utensil, a water cup, when he saw

a child drink from his hands – most of us still want to enjoy the hot latte. Prosperity and generation of wealth are results of working with the natural laws of the universe while having awareness of that which is within. Achieving an abundant state is an exercise in self-belief and an expression that we are limitless beings and *already* abundant. We already *have* everything; we're just stepping into a vision of abundance here on earth.

The key to successful manifestation – to making what's in our minds into reality – is to know, at a very deep level, that you already have everything. Of all the messages I regularly convey, this is by far the most problematic for people to absorb and put to work in their lives. That alone says quite a bit about our self-imposed blockages to our own success. Why is it so difficult to believe that we are inherently abundant, trusting we can easily lead a life of wealth and prosperity? It's because we still don't get who we are. We are all one, meaning that we are composed of perfect, limitless substance. That means we already *are* everywhere. We don't need to feel a lack of ownership of anything, because we already own everything. You can throw a party, celebrate, feel colossal joy knowing you have it all. You *are* the All. And the All is so almost inconceivably abundant that we can marvel at the sheer size of the idea. In short, the Divine has made it impossible for you to be anything but abundant.

Feeling fuller, richer, plentiful, happier, or beloved is just a way we like to demonstrate our innate knowingness of being the All, which is our natural state of abundance. Often when we surrender to life, and are relaxed in a peaceful state of mind, we can operate in this conceptual realm with very little effort. A blue sky fills us to the brink, we imagine a global community of souls working together, and suddenly everything is seen through a loving lens. In theory, the big picture makes sense and

> I put all my good thoughts into the person I'm working on. I feel I am bringing my spiritual side into that person.
>
> *Sharon, massage therapist*

there's a kinship with spirit. During those moments, we feel the benefits of existing within a perpetual state of the All.

However, in a physical world, it's easier said than done. It would require 24/7 spiritual awareness – even when we are doing the laundry, which seems nearly impossible. But creatively demonstrating the All in a physical world is everyone's fundamental soul work. It's the underlying assumption supporting our prosperity consciousness. In other words, if we want to demonstrate the All by letting our abundance flow, whether through sales, a stock portfolio, volunteer work, or creating a home, we can absolutely achieve abundance as a result of those efforts. What's required?

EXPECT CHALLENGES

Abundance in the form of material wealth, beautiful relationships, or peace of mind is *not* a result of luck; it is a mental, emotional, and spiritual discipline, not limited but enhanced by worldly conditions. In spite of our perceived limitations, we can channel our energies into the right places. Earth is the premier university of expression – it's a taxing environment in which to express the true self. We are not deprived by circumstances; we've sculpted our own stumbling blocks in order to learn different ways to create reality. Some conditions are created at the soul level prior to arrival; others we get into fairly well during our earth time. Many of us have outlined more difficult problems to overcome for the purpose of evolving our soul, which is why we must stop comparing our lives with others'. Everyone chooses different issues to work through.

Learn to view life, with all its contradictions and strife, as a blessing because it presents another opportunity to *create*. You came here to practice being like the Divine, who is the ultimate idea of creation. Your process of creation will challenge your perceptions, but view your mishaps like door swings. When one channel for energy closes, another opens so that the system can remain in balance. That is a natural law. The energy of life always finds a way, no matter how tough the going gets.

Creating anything, whether it is a product, situation, or idea, is always an expression of our core, fundamental energy. All life and whatever we desire is already here. It's just in another energy form, and we can translate that form into something else we want. When we create or generate outward appearance, we harness the primary impulse of the universe and express something new with the same energy that presently exists. We use what we already own, but with a personalized, unique soul-stamp. Is it easy? No! This exercise gets top ranking on everyone's inventory of greatest frustrations. Why?

Since our natural state of being is spirit, I believe we are much more in tune with energy work on the other side: an existence without limits, where thoughts can be instantly manifested. We do not associate limitation with perfection, as limitation is a human idea, not a divine one. One of everyone's biggest gripes about earth life is that we can't manifest what we want as quickly as we'd like – whether it is perfect health, an education, success, or even friends. At a subconscious level, it's annoying to just about everyone on the planet.

We're not accustomed to the limited human speed of our own thought process, made even slower by the weight of negativity, old programming, and everyday distractions. So we start off attempting to prosper by being frustrated by the less-than-speedy physical results of what we mentally fashion. Add that to other disappointments, such as the perception of not being in the immediate presence of the pure love of God, and homesickness for heaven. Those three can be a foundation of depression and illness, especially when we allow ourselves to get stuck there.

In short, no matter what you believe about life on the other side, practice patience every day. Stedman Graham, a CEO who

> Everybody in my building needs me. I get thanked all day long. I know I am needed here.
>
> *Pat, janitor*

speaks about leadership and empowerment, once said that the greatest equalizer for everyone on the planet is that we have the same twenty-four hours, meaning everyone has to operate within the same framework of time. It's true: *everyone* is subject to the same constraint. Overachievers and working women, take note: prepare to take the warp factor down a few notches. Demonstrating abundance is *not* a race.

Let's resign ourselves. When it comes to manifesting what we want on earth, we're all in the same boat, but we can begin to paddle together by just being smart and lovable and recognizing that an unlimited spirit needs and wants to be at work in the world *through* us. Spirit wants us to prosper – and there is no rea-

> I can only make the burgers so fast. People are in such a hurry – I wish I could wave a magic wand and "poof!" . . . instant food!
>
> *Theresa, employee,*
> *fast-food chain*

son to think we can't be successful at raising the collective consciousness in the process. We *can* make positive change in the world. It only takes practice! Remember, we are the All and you are your true self. You already are abundant cosmic material, perfectly qualified to experience success.

While time, speed, and everyday constraints are part of our world, they don't permanently block our ability to demonstrate an abundant life. To craft a loving and prosperous life, we must first acknowledge our physical existence and wholeheartedly embrace it. As much as we'd like to think a thing instantly into being, it's highly unlikely to happen, unless we're wizards. Meditating all day, willing money, a spectacular house, a different job, or even a meaningful relationship to manifest, will usually not produce grand results. The rules of physics are unavoidable, as are its rules of engagement. We can have a vision of a new house, but we're going to need blueprints and contractors. We can't get a return on investment until we learn the basic concepts of business and the marketplace, or even how to balance a checkbook. Learning the rules of money and the most logical way to get a job done is part of the program, along with pitching in a big dose of our own efforts to make it happen.

In short, we've got to *move* if we want to move mountains, and the first step is learning the earth rules. Begin to create success by bringing forth what you already have: your innate, individual talents, a good dose of true self-awareness, and the desire to enhance both by using life's experiences positively and productively. Don't be alarmed by how much time it takes, be patient, and embrace your challenges. Constraints are always there for our own benefit. Underneath it all, you are the All. And that means you are, and always will be, unlimited in what you can do.

Divine power has always been within you – it's just waiting to be released. Make a commitment to permanently disassembling the mental logjams you've acquired over this idea and allow your true self to flow like a downriver current. Better yet, skip the canoe ride altogether and opt to fly instead. Use any opportunity to identify with your unlimited nature. Next time someone asks, "Who are you?" reply, "I am the unlimited energy of the universe. I can prosper anywhere." It's far more accurate and self-loving than stating your name, what you do, or where you live.

Limiting Beliefs Block Abundance

If we resonate with the idea of our unlimited nature, why do we still have trouble paying bills or obtaining material possessions? What holds us captive? An enormous boulder standing in the way of our abundance arises from old assumptions about how results are achieved: getting ahead means taking away from others, lying, doing whatever it takes to make the next sale, adopting a more aggressive pace, or dictating how miracles will arrive. Another stagnating belief is that lack exists, which is simply not true. We waste far too much energy thinking about lack, which is the biggest obstacle to our own abundance. There is no mysteriously limited quantity of energy, the basic form from which everything arises. Energy is limitless.

We also deny our inherent talents in favor of a more logical option, a safer choice, or what our parents want us to do. Then our gift, which is the easiest channel for our abundance, falls by the wayside. Every person on this planet has a talent to offer the world: nobody lacks gifts. Too often, we compare ourselves to others and expect an identical level of prosperity. Vow to stop wasting your energy to demonstrate prosperity like that of your sister, your brother, or the neighbors. You have an entirely different soul objective and are meant to pursue a unique path. Choose to focus on your own self-development. Learn to have confidence in your matchless capabilities. Put your work efforts into a loving, positive course of action that will benefit others, doing exactly what you love to do, and you will make money. It's inevitable.

Above all, quit thinking about lack. Whatever you focus your energy on is what you will receive. Begin to replace negative, limiting thoughts with ones of prosperity and abundance. Think about what you *do* want, not what you don't want, no matter what your present circumstances. Visualize yourself in a present situation having exactly what you desire. Stop worrying about how much money everyone else has and how they get it.

It's no surprise that money is an idea that often carries a negative and limiting connotation. Money is merely a medium of exchange for goods and services; it is your energy made visible. It's not evil, unclean, or tempting. Don't equate money with greed, exploitation, selfishness, or lack for someone else. Equate money with freedom, goodwill, and generosity – the spiritual values of money. Believe that money is an expression of you and your unlimited God-self. Since money is energy, use it to express your feelings, words, and thoughts. Be generous without denying yourself what you need. Use money for right action; use it to help others. You can begin to release obstacles to your own abundance if you attach these ideas to each time you spend money and if you believe that it returns to you like a boomerang.

Another common limiting belief about money is that it *causes* prosperity in your life. Money is not the cause of abundance, it is an *effect*. If you place all your focus into the effect and don't recognize the cause, you are limiting your ability to generate more money. When illness is treated successfully, the cause is addressed, and not the symptoms. The effects indicate there is something wrong with the system. With money, seeing yourself as profitable is a positive image, but put an equal amount of energy into the idea which represents the foundation of money: your unlimited spiritual substance, or your true supply. Think of your true supply as a wildly abundant universe and the energy of money as your spiritual consciousness. That is a major change in attitude you'll need to allow form to appear and manifest more money in your life.

SET NEW MENTAL EQUIVALENTS

Sometimes old belief systems must change in order to create a new reality. Limiting beliefs, just like positive, empowering thoughts, provide a foundation for our experiences and what we demonstrate, not just in the business world, but in our personal lives as well. Old beliefs can leave us behind. Often they are stale ideas left over from our childhood experiences or from other areas of life that no longer carry any useful meaning. Abandoning negative assumptions about lack opens room to develop an abundant mindset. We can do that by setting a new mental equivalent that resets the dial to our trust channel – the channel we listen to that tells us to trust that we already have it all.

Emmet Fox, a "new thought" minister and author in the 1940s, stressed the importance of "setting a mental equivalent" to create an abundant life, borrowing the term from chemistry and physics. For example, engineers must work out the equivalent of heat in order to determine how much energy it represents in the form of another energy. They can determine the amount of fuel it takes to drive an engine and how much processing energy it takes to produce the fuel.

> I kept telling my kids, "You are what you are inside." They can do anything they believe in, be anyone they choose to be in their life. I hope they remember that.
>
> *Kristi, mother of three teenagers*

A mental equivalent is a wonderful metaphor for our work in instituting positive change in our lives and world. Like engineers, we can create the equivalent of every experience or object in the physical world by changing the thought to which it corresponds.

Scientifically, we've accepted that one kind of energy translates into another to produce the same effect. Everything on earth is energy anyway. All matter, when it's broken down into subatomic particles, is energy. This book is energy, the dog is energy, you are energy. The same is true for the energy of thought. To attract goodness, you must set a mental equivalent of goodness by accepting that you are worthy of receiving good, visualizing it, and feeling the goodness coming to you. Simple – and probably what your mother told you in third grade. If you want prosperity, wealth, happiness, that is where you must spend time mentally, not once a week but *all* the time.

Fox taught that whatever you want in life – a satisfying job, healthy body, friends, opportunities – you must first set a mental equivalent to attract it. If you have something you want to get rid of – ill health, strife, or poverty – then first get rid of the mental equivalent by striking out the belief that those ideas and experiences must be part of your world and the world at large. Shed your old mental equivalent skin. Then you will begin to make change, not just for yourself but for others around you.

Feel what you want with tremendous emotion, be grateful, rejoice in the abundance of everything. Notice joy and prosperity everywhere, be thankful to be part of an incredible, universal spiritual equation of such magnificent complexity that you are humbled by its awesomeness. Think gigantic. Set the bar as high as you want: there is no reason to feel limited, because your true nature makes that impossible anyway. Don't be fearful of living, of failure, of the future. You already know how unproductive fear can be, as our collective consciousness has translated fear over the millennia into a belief in lack, poverty, and illness.

Practice Clarity and Interest

Fox's concept of mastery included two key principles he called clarity and interest. An abundant life is derived from the ability to mentally straddle the line between *clarity*, or knowing exactly what you want and believing you are already in receipt of it, and *interest*, or the emotional feelings you have about what you want. People generally have a problem with clarity. There's an old saying, "If you don't know where you're going, any road will get you there." In other words, by not knowing exactly what you want or how you define your success and dreams, you can take any path and wander indefinitely. You'll receive exactly what you've asked for, and that is a nebulous vision of success and dreams. First homework assignment in Principles of Manifestation: ask for what you want. Visualize it clearly and revisit the idea often.

An error people frequently make is that they articulate what they want in great detail, but they lack passion or belief in the idea. Part two of Fox's abundance formula means you must be sincerely interested in what you want, and emotional about seeing yourself within the idea. You must absolutely *love* what you want, love your vision passionately, feel it deeply, embrace it, live and breathe it. That is how something becomes part of you. It's how you claim it as your own.

There's plenty of evidence that clarity and interest exist, courtesy of people who speak with clarity about every ache and pain they have. They relive their surgical procedures in great detail and hold court in their living room to get you to connect empathically with their disease. They've claimed permanent ownership of their mishap by speaking with zest about their physical condition. They can't let it go; consequently, they continue to spin that reality for themselves. They've done a fabulous job of creating an abundantly unhealthy mindset, where the body begins to adopt what the mind has established.

Overall, abundance is a spiritual principle requiring a pure motive. Abundance is a deeply spiritual lesson because it is about knowing that the presence within you constitutes your supply, which is your true source of power. It's about attuning to the true self and channeling those energies to create something that serves your higher good, not about creating physical realities that serve no useful purpose.

If you think about having great amounts of wealth by planning a store robbery with clarity and interest, you could easily make it happen, although it doesn't constitute true abundance. Money never lasts if obtained by force or through deceitful means. Your experiences, as well as the physical objects you manifest, are effects of your thinking because they all flow through your belief system. Greed, selfishness, war, lack, bad economic conditions, or struggle can be manifested if that's what is present in the mind.

We are always told not to judge by appearances. Why? Because the appearance has no value in itself. Nothing is what it seems on the outside: the effect has those attributes that you give it and nothing else. When we look behind an appearance, we look through it to the truth that lies behind it. As soon as the spiritual truth is evident to us, the appearance changes. This is the mental world that Fox spoke of, not the material world.

The material world is fabulous when we channel the good side of the force. We don't have to punish ourselves through starvation, poverty, self-abuse, or religious fervor. Material life *is* sacred: it's about matter. You matter. It's about our earth, our opportunities, and what we can create from our mental state – hopefully, something absolutely wonderful. We simply must remember to stay in balance and work with both principles, the mental and the material, while knowing that we *do* live, underneath our appearances, in a mental and spiritual world.

MAKE DECISIVE CHOICES ANCHORED IN THE PRESENT MOMENT

Transferring energy, or a vision, into manifested form is a very old biblical lesson. How can two fish and five loaves feed an entire community? By clarity and interest, but also by choice. Choice is the action we take to make it happen. It's our free will to dictate a course of action – we can't wait and ponder decisions endlessly. If you feel that you want to manifest a new opportunity with deep emotion, and are thankful for knowing that it already exists at a fundamental energy level, you've just created it by making a decisive choice.

I recently met someone on a retreat who spent years analyzing what she wants. Divorced twice, and weary from a career spent in the health-care field, she finally sketched out a wonderful plan to shift her natural healing efforts into massage therapy and medical consulting. She was ready to move into a new apartment and enter a new, personal discovery phase with a great sense of humor and determination. Her new choices had a great deal of emotion attached; she was jubilant about the potential changes that could arrive in her life and the prosperity that would result.

But for the entire week of the retreat she backtracked, spending an enormous amount of energy dwelling on the past. She sought verbal confirmation from everyone in the group that her former path had been the best course of action at the time, set within circumstances of severe limitation. All the years of single parenting, financial struggle, workplace strife, and marital difficulties began to churn around the issue of justifying her new path. Instead of using the time to rest and building energy reserves to move forward, she drained herself and dwindled the energy of others in the group by vacillating between past and present choices. By the end of the retreat, she had lost her clear vision by depending upon everyone else to push her forward with approval.

> Most of the time I spend with people, they are living in the past. The past has such a powerful hold on those who get stuck there permanently. I'm constantly dragging people back into the present.
>
> *Anita, therapist*

I genuinely believe she will accomplish her goals, but not until she achieves clarity on what she chooses as a new course of action and shakes free of the past. For some, the past serves as nothing more than an illustration of how they have successfully demonstrated limitation. Most of us have had this lesson, it's nothing to be embarrassed about, and we certainly don't need to engage in a lot of self-flagellation over it. But if you never choose, or keep questioning what you choose until you've forgotten why you're choosing to change your present circumstances, you don't have to face disappointment – and that's a very safe place to be.

CHOOSE CONSCIOUSLY WITH GUSTO

Living in a democracy, we often herald the benefits of having choices, but we often forget the gusto that should accompany choosing. We are free to choose within very large parameters and have a huge amount of opportunity, but it's really not all about where we are born. Everyone, no matter where, is a soul with free will and has many avenues of choice despite adversity. Choice is a funny thing requiring a tremendous sense of self-centeredness and, at times, the wild abandon that accompanies the unexpected. Surprises may land on our path along the way, and if we don't have a good attitude about the surprise, we aren't experiencing choice as a creative exercise.

Entrepreneurs will gladly share business tales from the front about how many times, after a careful analysis, they chose an unprofitable path of action that made it difficult to put one foot in front of the other. In the choice department, we often experience the business mindset because we become cautious; we lean toward cynicism and wind up watering down our visions with self-doubt, keeping no-nonsense decisions on the balance sheet with a rigid practicality. We soon conclude, "I can accomplish only if I choose correctly." And then, unfortunately, past failures become a deadweight around abundance and prosperity, and our confidence that we can manifest what we desire plummets.

Our sacred gift is the *power of choice* we have to accomplish our desires in any creative and loving way we see fit, despite our circumstances. Choice is a good thing and we must use it fearlessly, artfully, with a great deal of passion and self-belief. It's our earth job to plunge into uncharted waters and experience life, and at the same time to be clear about why we dove in and what we want. It's what we signed up for! Let's stop complaining. Get creative when you choose, let go of past baggage, be clear about what you want *now*, and feel it so deeply that you must raise your arms up in an expansive gesture of joyful thanks at knowing it is already part of your reality.

Remember, your true self is limitless, so make sure your dreams are equally big. Identify with limitlessness, *be* without limits. Live the idea of limitlessness by breathing in a love of life and exhaling gratitude, no matter how silly that may feel. Choose to go for what you believe in from the minute you get up in the morning until you fall asleep. Don't go for half the kingdom – go for the whole kingdom. Go for it in its entirety and incorporate the total knowingness of who you are into your entire expression – your work, your words, your world. Realize the presence of spirit within you and reclaim it, rejoice in it, love it, and know you are one gigantic, unlimited energy form that you can convert into anything you desire. Use your imagination. You can do it!

Take an Inventory of Faulty Thinking

Faulty thinking can be seen worldwide. The evidence is the collective belief system that influences how we think. It permeates all socio-economic groups, not just the privileged and powerful. The energy of thought is like the Michigan football stadium wave, picking up speed and intensity as more join in. When two or more gather in the name of an idea, it becomes a powerful force, an energy tool, no matter what the idea, good or bad. Once the wave gets going, replacing it with something better, or even reversing the action, is problematic. Unseating negative thoughts and setting new mental equivalents takes some time and practice, but it can be done. We *can* make the wave go the other way. The amount of effort will be up to us.

Unfortunately, a lot of worldly energy is expended in trying to take the shortcuts. Who wants to go through all that mental effort of changing our thinking and belief system about abundance? Most of us just get a job that will provide a nice living and spend our income and extra time outside the office having fun; we're not used to the pleasure we can have as a result of our true self-expression. Can you imagine the difference if our entire culture directed energy into utilizing everyone's individual, innate gifts? And encouraged the release of old, outdated ideas about our limited nature, choice, and lack? And what if we collectively set new mental equivalents? Perhaps we are years away from a workplace makeover derived from our positive thinking potential, but we can begin to institute change *now*, beginning with ourselves. In your own work environment, change your mindset by applying abundance principles to the bigger picture. Remember, we are all one collective consciousness, just as we are all one energy. We are helping others to unseat faulty thinking when we first unseat our own.

> I deal with cancer patients every day. After a while, I just run out of energy believing we can beat cancer. It's so overwhelming.
>
> *Maria, radiology technician*

To collectively create an abundant planet, we must take regular inventory as a world participant. Remember, everything in our nation is an embodiment of mental equivalents held by citizens; likewise, the state of the world embodies the mental equivalent of everyone living on earth. Humanity holds the mental equivalent of war because we believe in fear. We still hold on to the notion that we can enrich ourselves by taking from somebody else. Death and lack are not far behind. If we didn't believe in death and lack, we wouldn't have fear. Everything on the physical plane is a precipitation of a mental equivalent held by one or more people. If we have a mental equivalent of strife, we'll be quarrelsome wherever we go. If we want peace wherever we go, then we need to have the mental equivalent of peace. We have such tremendous power with our own mind and intentions – we really need little else to demonstrate our ideas, positive or negative. We are, in fact, what we think, whether we think that way or not.

Why Don't We See Our Abundant World?

Whether you adopt Emmet Fox's worldview or your own rendition to change your perception on prosperity, a little analysis can make a difference in your transition to a positive mindset. Let's examine five negative traps that detract from a prosperous vision.

We are addicted to negativity. The media facilitates the perception of a limited world. As we are all television viewers conditioned by what we are told, we don't see the value in positive thinking and we don't see the power of our own minds to make change. It's difficult to cultivate our positive side when we're so frequently thrown off track with celebrity obsession, character assassination, prodding and probing into people's lives on reality TV, unsubstantiated investigative reporting, and the recent phenomenon of young people ingesting live worms and insects. Positive doesn't sell on network prime time; problems do.

Not all networks and newspapers carry negative programming, but a great many have brought examples of the very worst mental equivalents into our homes. You've noticed how reading the paper or watching the morning news before breakfast sets a tone throughout the day, especially in a raised heart rate; the news has become a necessity on par with the morning double-mocha skim cap. The grisly gatekeepers of the media have a very bad habit of focusing on what we want to dismiss – the negative aspects of life – in the pre- and post-dinner hour. Why? Negativity and crisis get our attention, war sells, lack and limited resources bring you back after the commercial, thereby increasing the rates for ad time. There's sizzle in scandal and gang wars, and very few treetop cats make it to the news desk. Fictitious violent action heroes keep us going until midnight. According to the ratings, this is what motivates us into action and loving-kindness. The strategy: showcase a slice of life we're *not* supposed to choose.

I suppose pointing out our faults in chorus is a good reminder of the work that needs to be done here on earth. But the problem is that we've turned even our most noble acts to better the world into a political agenda by using them to manipulate popular opinion. Sadly, there is a lack of understanding of where true power is obtained, and as a consequence, we've been conditioned to pay attention to the worst in life.

We think there's something wrong with abundance. North Americans are full of conflict about our own abundance. We desire a prosperous life but feel there's something wrong with success. We seem to be easily convinced by a few pundits in the media that it's not acceptable to have until everyone has the same thing, and if you have, then someone has to do without. As individuals, we feel lousy about our success after a barrage of political tut-tutting about how we should not have more than the next person. Very non-abundant programming.

We are also conflicted as a society, feeling that abundance has negative connotations. Prosperity and abundance are equated in financial terms, and we believe that everyone wants the same version of prosperity, which is not true. Abundance has varied definitions and is evident within every segment of the socio-economic spectrum. Many who have a multitude of friends, jobs they love, peace of mind, or a service they perform for humanity feel abundant in ways that have little to do with income.

In a world that has lack and poverty, we do not look at the big picture often enough. *Everyone* is on a self-development path of their own choosing, and soul journeys will differ. Remember, others are helping you elevate your consciousness as well – and the dynamic of what we see in the world, which does include evil and poverty, is there by our own design. Of course, we've blown it on many fronts, but it's never too late to get it right. We can pick up the pieces and help others achieve a sense of self-worth and economic autonomy. We can educate, love, lend a hand, inspire, and help others reach a dream. *Everyone* has something important to give. Above all, know that every situation in life is one we have designed by our own mental mindset, but we can choose a different course of action. It *is* possible to change.

Abundance has been a major source of resentment on the part of people who have made some bad choices. To compensate, their proposed solution is to redistribute society's wealth to make everyone abundant – which just raises the likelihood that the class war will continue indefinitely. In the nightly polarizing debate on taxes, we see a skewed view of prosperity based upon a belief in lack, a belief in limited opportunity, and a fear of success. If we spent less time as a society arguing about where we were twenty years ago, and more time unseating our faulty thinking about leading an abundant life today, we'd have a collective mental revolution, which just might unseat some political views on how to redistribute the wealth. What we need is more awareness of positive, abundant thinking through a continent-wide seminar on our unlimited, spiritual nature. Then *everyone* would have to move forward.

We should be empowered by the abundance we achieve and not feel shameful about it, viewing it as a tremendous opportunity to show love. We live in an abundant society, capable of instituting positive change at a worldwide level in the area of stabilizing nations and promoting free speech and human rights. That's not so bad. We're not going to do everything perfectly, as most policy is simply trial and error. Pundits lead us to believe that we should expect to completely mend our nations, and the world dynamic, at every election. We've got to stop beating ourselves up for our abundance – and for the speed with which we

> Hearing that TV news all the time just makes it worse. There's so much life to live, you gotta just believe it's better than we see.
>
> *Margaret, seventy-nine years young*

can get others to translate our ideas into their reality.

Our society is also market-driven. Capitalism has rules to operate within, and that's not such a bad thing, because it offers us a great deal of creativity and freedom. It was not designed to give a good case of the guilts to those who have done well. Abundance as a result of capitalism has been shamed by environmental groups who want to stop industrialization in favor of saving the earth. Who isn't in favor of protecting our beautiful planet? If we heard more stories on the nightly news about the latest advancement in clean technologies, or how communities are partnering with industry on waste issues, and about the newfangled energy-efficient homes and cars, we'd be better informed about the good works of those who are attempting to rebalance science and nature. Our society would be grooming a new generation of architects and engineers and cultivating a market for services that would help solve environmental issues that we've *globally* created.

Prosperity isn't ruining the earth, our attitude is. We need to get our consumption level at a sustainable rate in all economic sectors and quit wasting time and energy figuring out who did the most damage. It's everyone's challenge, not just those who are doing well financially. And prosperous big business is not always our nemesis. We need to address the individual lack of focus on living with our mind, body, and spirit in balance.

We don't want responsibility for our lives. The new societal disease is irresponsibility, not just in epidemic proportions among teenagers but throughout all age groups and walks of life. It's so much easier to let someone else take the blame for our lack of abundance. The workforce provides an amazing cross-section of people who won't take responsibility. As an employer, I have seen it all, and I have been skunked more times than I can count by people who can't finish anything, who won't step up to the plate when the going gets tough, or who don't want to learn a new skill.

Work culture has never been viewed as a spiritual self-development opportunity that allows us to strengthen our resolve, test our limits, or improve society. But, truly, work is an opportunity to contribute to everyone's good and a chance to express the gift of self. For too long we have viewed work only as an activity that generates money, and not as an expression of our gifts. If we cared more about the expression, and less about the money, we'd be more successful doing exactly what we want to do and are good at doing, and that very success would be a fundamental building block of prosperity.

Our work patterns are also largely influenced by a mobile work culture and an ability to just keep moving on, if the going gets rough. We're not learning to reflect about what it means when we get fired or can't get along with our colleagues. As a culture, we are failing to correlate abundance with responsibility. I've seen many employees drag their low self-esteem into the workplace; they have an opportunity to develop confidence and feelings of success by simply accepting the collective outcome of what is produced, but they don't want to be evaluated. They feel threatened and unsafe when they are held accountable, so they just head off to the next job, blaming their bosses or work environment. They don't take any mental inventory and keep moving on to the next situation, wondering why they don't feel or see more prosperity in their lives.

As a society of teachers, parents, and employers, we are failing to cultivate the idea that work and personal development are highly integrated. The work environment is part of our soul school and is actually a fantastic testing ground for our ideas about how we use our God/Goddess power – not just managers and presidents, but everyone. Most organizational leaders would agree: if people would stick around long enough to take responsibility for bad decisions, they would grow wiser and more valuable to their team. It's inspiring to see someone grow and be able to pass their knowledge on to everyone else. We don't trust the deeper implications of owning up to our mistakes. Taking responsibility for our own lives equals our abundance potential, at work or home.

We are also a culture confused about the spiritual theme of responsibility. We don't spend enough time thinking about who or what is responsible for our lives, and we are afraid to make the conceptual leap. Some accept that the Divine sketches out our entire lifetimes, making sense of a rich or poor life. From this viewpoint, the Divine has bestowed good fortune upon you. If you're rich, it's meant to be. But if you allow that premise to propel your life exclusively, then you are also accepting that the Divine has prescribed the sheer poverty of third world countries and starving children, people who have no money for lifesaving operations, and oppressed women who live hand-to-mouth. Circumstance seems to have sealed their fate. As we work to remediate such so-called divinely prescribed situations here on earth, we feel as if we are emptying an entire ocean of lack with a tablespoon. How can perfect creators be so unfair in assigning prosperity?

Accepting responsibility begins with a desire to view life as an undulating, multimedia event designed by many, both human and divine. We help create our own self-development path and are responsible for what happens. If everyone has a hand in designing their abundance lesson at a soul level, then some sense can be made of poverty. But once we get here, we are *all* responsible for overcoming poverty, lack, pain, and suffering created by either past lifetimes or current actions. We see the effects of our own designs: our governments, our purchasing power, our faulty thinking. To alleviate suffering and create world abundance, we need to pitch in. We must take responsibility, using our gifts to help create jobs, good health, or anything else we deem valuable. It's the only way we're going to evolve our souls.

We think abundance is impossible because there are not enough resources. We are confused about limited resources and tend to focus on conservation because industrialized nations are gobbling up the landscapes, endangered species, air, and water at alarming rates. The world seems to be shrinking as its population grows, and a big backyard is just not what it used to be. It is becoming difficult to unseat the concept of a limited supply – after all, there's only so much petroleum to go around, right? Our energy consumption alone leads to an abundant lifestyle. We've been told that this means we exist at the expense of others.

However, our perceptions of limitation, and of limits to growth, are maturing since Dennis Meadows wrote the book on the subject. There is no lack at the fundamental level. In the big picture, the issue is neither the staggering effects of our consumption nor the competition over resources. The truth is that there is plenty to go around; we just haven't figured out how to redesign our energy systems and resource use to distribute it. Our immediate problem is our inability to live in an equilibrium state with what we have; it's not that we don't have enough. There's a big difference in those two assumptions. We have not learned to manage our consuming lifestyles and live in harmony with the planet, getting everyone on board in the process. We choose to live out of balance.

We have old programming on the concept of deserving. Since my parents experienced the shortages of depression and rationing in wartime, money and abundance have been carefully guarded ideas. For those who survived, one person's wealth translated into lack for another. Even though my parents were hardworking and generous people, I never once heard them say they deserved wealth because there was enough wealth in the world for everyone to enjoy, no matter what. They adopted their own ideas of what abundance meant and created their own comfort zone by reinforcing what was wrong with people who *did* have money.

In my world, people who had a lot of money were ascribed negative qualities: rich, snotty, bossy, nose in the air. Not having money meant you were down-to-earth, grounded, in touch with real life, approachable, good, and wholesome – those were valued qualities in people. By the time I struck out on my own, I had living on a budget down pat. But I carried so many negative assumptions about having money that I had no confidence I could ever fit into the circles of people who enjoyed great wealth, should I be lucky enough to stumble into them.

Childhood conditioning on abundance, especially money, is often passed down from families who suffered by experiencing severe states of lack. As each generation moves further away from the depression era's anxiety about stockpiling money (because there might not be any later), we will eventually cycle out of old thinking.

> I think being rich is about your family and everyone who loves you. Without that, I'd never know how to enjoy my paycheck. It's what it's all about.
>
> *Penny, marketing representative*

Additionally, early messages we receive that relate to our value as individuals, such as gender stereotypes, have a lot to do with our feelings of abundance. For example, if you were born female and told as a little girl that you could never be as worthy as a boy, and your parents praised the achievements and qualities of boys but not girls, that would change the way you approached life. Your deep-seated feelings of deserving – whether in regard to food, choosing a partner, or the way you manage your finances or career – would inform your life. Often we believe we don't deserve an abundant life filled with love and goodness because we have not received enough positive messages growing up. It's time to clean house and get rid of old programming. Let nothing stand between you and an abundant life, certainly not old, outdated, insignificant ideas from others that have no bearing on the path you currently travel.

But before you call your parents and tell them they blew it when they raised you, keep in mind that everyone, by the nature of their beautiful light within, helps to challenge your perception of what can be. Reach out, love those who taught you, and thank them for being your teachers. Be grateful you had an opportunity to develop strength. Extend yourself as far as you possibly can, and help others to overcome. By reaching out, you are connecting with everyone on the planet. And above all, be generous. By helping everyone else develop an abundant mindset, you are being given a chance to practice your own mental and spiritual discipline. Be grateful that you live in a society where that is possible, and quit complaining about the state of the world. Get out there, expand consciousness, and express your true self.

Develop Prosperity Consciousness Through Labyrinth Thinking

Having good imagery helps to unseat ideas that are no longer useful and provides focus to our intentions. Consider life as a journey through a labyrinth, not a maze. A maze is built inside a box and has many entrances and exits, giving us a choice of paths. However, mazes have dead ends and elaborate twists, turns, and alleys. In the traditional understanding, a labyrinth, combining the imagery of a circle and a spiral, has a meandering, purposeful path to the center. To find the labyrinth's center, there is only one path in and out with one choice presented: enter and walk the path, or remain outside.

Why is it helpful to apply labyrinth thinking to reach prosperity consciousness? Because we already know life is an infinite journey. The labyrinth is a metaphor for the universal superstructure we operate within – it offers an exercise in personal growth. Each time we retreat and take self-inventory, we can go deeper within and come out with something new, whether it's a refreshed attitude or greater spiritual awareness. It's the cyclical outlook on life that keeps us coming back to the center, to our self. There will never be an end to the process, only different venues with more elaborate choices. And our experiences are for our own benefit; otherwise, how would we learn to reach our own potential?

Having prosperity consciousness means that each time we vocalize what we want in our lives, we have to cooperate with spirit and not just wait for it to happen. Action opens the flow. We *must* have the courage to walk. Always be aware of who you are and listen to your higher self. Everything you experience outside the labyrinth is a reflection of your inner world of thoughts and feelings. As within, so without. As above, so below. In the world around you, consciously and unconsciously, you are demonstrating what is in your heart and mind. The more clearly you understand who you are and your journey, the greater results you'll see.

Build a New Mental Equivalent for Abundance

As I've been through numerous financial ups and downs of enormous proportions, I've laid claim to every Dances with Wolves name on the prosperity continuum, from "Completely Broke Without Car" to "Stands with a Fistful." During my very long tour on the not-having side, I witnessed the disastrous effects of negative thinking in my own life. Nothing teaches better than experience. Past negative programming, enhanced by a dose of low self-esteem and a loose grip on the true self, is the number one recipe for non-success in all areas of life. And, as the years go on, it picks up strength.

In my life, old, ingrained money messages left over from my parents took center stage. Prosperity was a result of having a dependable job that guaranteed security, not necessarily what you love to do. And if you achieved an abundant state – well, you'd better not show that too much, because it meant that lack might be evident in others' lives. "Having" translated into lack for someone else, which we were taught to feel guilty about. Hiding abundance and success, even while building it bit by bit, soon translated into taking pride in "not having." These attitudes created a foundation for my financial experiences and feelings of success for many years. I held myself back, afraid to take charge. Although I believe I scheduled these lessons for my own soul development in order to overcome limitation, this old baggage did weigh me down and forced me to spend a lot of time on personal growth.

Years later, when my husband's lackluster company was millions of dollars in debt, an almost inconceivable situation, despite our honest efforts to repair it, we realized that the years spent on a tight budget would not turn it around. After deeply examining his core beliefs, we realized Tom was also holding himself back. He had adopted a monk archetype, completely content to be without material possessions. His generosity toward everyone, albeit his most lovable quality, was also his nemesis, leading him to make business decisions that seemed right for some individuals but not necessarily for the organization as a whole. He also believed he did not deserve wealth, and he did not have confidence in his ability to shift mental patterns to turn a bad financial situation around.

Tom's non-deserving mindset was similar to mine. It was *not* the right formula for an owner of a company that was responsible for hundreds of people's jobs and benefits. Neither of us knew how to harness our unlimited creative power. Our intentions to build a successful company were overshadowed by too many mental distractions. Besides, neither one of us had an awareness of the presence within; therefore we could not allow it to fully fill our consciousness. We relied upon prayer but were confused: how could we be thankful when each year the numbers took another down-ward plunge?

Many years later I realized that our intellectual vision took so long to manifest because we had set our sights too low and our bar too high. We had neither clarity nor interest – the powerful emotions to back up what we wanted. We were not deeply attuned to knowing the unlimited supply of the Divine and constantly looked for reasons why we couldn't rise above limitation. And we never spent any time sharing ideas of what *being* unlimited, in a universal sense, really meant. Basically, we were a couple of battered business cynics.

For each of us, there was a complete disconnect between clearly knowing what we wanted and visualizing it. We had to change our thinking to value our vision. We had to keep working with a great deal of faith. And we had to be deeply thankful for the abundance that we knew was already there without seeing any immediate results.

Starting over was not an option, as we had undertaken an enormous amount of financial risk. So instead we spent a considerable time analyzing the spiritual aspects of abundance and adopted a new mental equivalent. It was a mental and spiritual discipline. Every evening for six months, we shared stories and steps we were each taking to correct our thinking, especially about debt. We described our mental panorama of collective success. We visualized, feeling our success with great emotion. And we thanked in advance for a company we believed to be already wildly successful.

In the process, we discovered that the concept of debt challenges our belief system the most. Taking on debt is about having trust, because you believe the universe will provide you with an opportunity to generate income. Charge cards or even house mortgages, for that matter, are about the confidence of knowing you can pay bills at a later date. We kept our powder dry, operating in cash for everything except the business and our home, because it helped to focus our efforts into changing our belief system about our debt and how a universal, unlimited supply existed.

We turned the company around in about a year. Tom achieved enormous success by attracting an account that, at the time, we had no idea would become part of the financial aspect of the business. Many years later Tom sold the company for a very nice profit, realizing the completion of a big lesson in manifestation: it's not what you see, it's what you think. And abundance is not determined by outside conditions, the economy, war, or location. It's a state of mind.

You already know enough at this moment to create what you want in your life, money included, because money is a reflection of what is in your head. It's not luck, it's a mental process, energized by your emotions and the action you take to keep going forward. It's about the discipline of positive thinking and knowing you are unlimited because your supply is unlimited.

When you accept that you are unlimited in what you can accomplish, you will no longer fear the world you have been born into, nor the families who you think restrict your opportunities or personal growth, or even having your business take a turn for the worse. You will realize that the world is a gigantic canvas for your ideas and experiences. Even though the path you've set to discover them may be littered with rocks, there is *always* the opportunity to awaken to your own potential.

GIVE MORE THANKS TO IDENTIFY WITH YOUR SOURCE

I've learned that each time I experience lack and limitation, the universe is challenging me to demonstrate my true self. It is an opportunity to remain an empowered, open channel, and it prevents me from withdrawing from life. I actually stop focusing on money and success, and concentrate on my self-image as the pure demonstration of lavish abundance that will be me forever – that part of me that flows from consciousness. I let go of what people think, of what they say, of my desire to be on the cover of *Newsweek* enlightening millions of readers. I let it all go and instead focus on my authentic self, shedding my negative beliefs by viewing my limiting situation as it is: a consequence of a faulty belief system. Then I surrender to my unlimited nature and claim the source as my own, inventing a new image in my mind for resolving the issue. I give thanks, because the very origin of all prosperity thinking is a deep feeling of gratitude.

Often, it's difficult to demonstrate what you want without seeing it, and it's even more difficult to generate thanks for something you don't see. Remember, everyone's supply is constantly replenished, like a fruit-bearing tree. We don't have any concern when a healthy tree appears to be barren of leaves, because we know the fruit is within. We aren't concerned because the work is being done, whether we see it or not. A tree reminds us that if you believe you have already received what you want, then you will have it, just as soon as the time is ripe. A familiar ritual is giving thanks for food we are about to eat. It's about first experiencing *mentally* that our expectations will be fulfilled before we *physically* experience what we desire.

When you are aware of the source within you, or the presence of the Divine, then spirit can fill your consciousness. The more deeply you embrace spirit, the more permanently etched that idea will be in your everyday life. You'll identify with spirit, the unlimited source of everything that exists in the universe. It is this energy that interprets itself as every experience or form you see in the world, such as money.

Most of us make a lot of mistakes when we equate money with abundance. Money is an effect; it is not your supply. The Divine is your supply, the cause of abundance. When you focus on money as the effect (happiness, great wealth) rather than the cause (the Divine is your true supply of happiness and great wealth), you shut off your supply.

The same is true of any other effect you want, even if you give thanks in advance for what you want. Your employer is not your supply, nor is your spouse, car, house, family, or investments. No person, place, or condition is your supply. When you focus on these things as the source of your power, you give your power away. Money is only a *symbol* of your inner supply; the consciousness of the spirit within you is your true supply. And if you are always conscious of that, you will always keep your abundance channel open, to whatever you think with great clarity and interest. And the money will appear.

Throughout our lives and throughout history, we see endless examples of fallen CEOs or dictators who have squandered billions of dollars from their companies or countries. These episodes tell me we still have the wrong intentions when we think of money, not that money is bad for us. Although some behaviors to obtain money are evidence of faulty thinking, money itself is not evil. It doesn't make you rude or unsympathetic to the plight of others, or prevent you from sharing. Those ideas we cultivate all on our own, whether we have one dollar or a billion. The challenge isn't generating enough money for everyone to be rich; it is to convince everyone that we are all capable of demonstrating that which is within.

> I thank God every day for what I have.
>
> *Kelisha, receptionist*

After we get the hang of thanking (before we've received our good) and identifying with our source, we can easily expand our belief system about what we deserve to have. How rich can we be? There are endless answers: as rich as our contentment level, or rich enough to expand our consciousness as far as we want. We can even use money to help others expand their consciousness. When we express the true self more fully and completely, we will become ultimately prosperous. The opportunity to do this is a reason to keep a heart of joyful thanksgiving every day.

Raising Your Vibration Through Affirmations

Everyone gets off track from time to time – it's normal and a consequence of living in a complex, stressful world. Attract abundance and maintain a good mental equivalent by raising your vibration. Raising your vibration means giving loving attention, or energy, to what you want. We get faster results by attuning to an idea of what we want and then *allowing* it to come into our lives, because we are already in a state of thankfulness that it is here. That is another reason we write affirmations in the present moment: there really isn't any other time in our lives that is important. Live in the now, thank in the now, love in the now, and allow prosperity to happen in the now, knowing it is already present.

When we concentrate on the effects of the world, rather than our supply, we lower our vibrational quality, making it much harder to demonstrate what we want. You've heard the concept of alignment and finding "center" from many spiritual teachers, achieved by chanting, prayer, meditation, chakra balancing, even martial arts or exercise. Those activities help raise your vibrational quality by helping you to identify or resonate with the true self, so that goodness can manifest. Essentially, you are attuning to your God-force. That is why in affirmations, we focus on the "I am" within us and align our vibrational quality with that of our God/Goddess energy.

We do a pretty job of cultivating our own negative programming and often bring to the table a lot of negative assumptions about money and abundance that lower our vibration. You might recognize these.

It was never meant for me to have money.

I'm poor but clean (or good, pure, happy, content).

If I want to lead a spiritual life and be closer to God, it means I must have to give everything up. I'll be like Christ (or Buddha, Rumi, Mohammed, Mother Teresa) because not having any material wealth means I am purer (or righteous, religious, going to get a better afterlife).

You can live a pure life only without material items.

I don't want to learn about how money works – I'll just let_____ _____ do it. I just want to spend money.

I only care about large sums of money. Why should I pick up a penny off the sidewalk?

It's not worth my time, so I'll just do a mediocre (or lousy) job. *This shows overall disrespect for your true supply when it's giving you an opportunity. Choose not to do the job instead!*

Prosperity means I have to take something away from someone else.

I can't enjoy wealth because I feel guilty.

I will never be able to afford that. *You are building a "can't afford" consciousness. You will bring more events and things into your life that you cannot afford.*

I can't imagine having a million dollars – I wouldn't know what to do with it.

If I had a million dollars, I'd give it all away.

If I become wealthy, why should I be generous? I struggled so long, I'm going to let everyone else know how it feels not to have anything.

People who have money are wealthy snobs.

Being rich is selfish. You can have too much money.

Rich people consume all the world's natural resources. I love the earth too much to be rich.

Money represents temptation and evil.

I don't deserve what I really want: _____.

I don't want this deal *not* to work out.
If you're constantly worried about lack, you'll attract it.

I just want to be rich.
This one is particularly self-defeating, because you'll spend your energy on getting the money without any focus on how to do it.

You won't be able to demonstrate the law of being with this type of mental muck. Start affirming that you are a prosperity magnet because you possess the boundless wealth of the universe *without exception*. Spend time raising your vibration. Say that you attract all good things today, not tomorrow or next week. Love yourself, praise your abilities in the present moment, and build feelings of confidence.

I am a prosperous, intelligent, capable individual who can do anything.

I deserve health, wealth, love, and happiness in my life. I thank the universe for my opportunities.

I pay my bills with love and joy…
Come on, you can do this one!
…I love that I have the ability to pay this bill, and I rejoice in the goods and services I have received as a result of this bill.
I see the abundance in the universe everywhere I go. I see it in myself.

I am a loving individual, who is part of unlimited creation; therefore, I am unlimited in what I can do.

I am my divine self and I choose to demonstrate my highest good. I prosper everywhere I go because I love life.

I am an open channel to receive my abundance from the universe. I am open to new opportunities.

Remain open to the possibility that the universe is infinitely more creative than you in choosing the channel for abundance to flow through. If you outline exactly how you want to receive your good, you are definitely giving the idea some clarity. But be flexible. Devising a mental equivalent to own the winning lottery ticket might be a way to manifest abundance, but you are limiting the avenues by which good can come to you. Likewise, it's great to visualize opening the front door to discover a huge basketful of money, but it is more likely that the universe will present prosperity through people and opportunities. Be attentive and keep your options open.

> When I do yoga, I think about filling my body with loving energy. Sometimes I notice that those are the days when almost everything goes right.
>
> Lynda, yoga instructor

Maintain high vibrational quality by practicing verbal harmlessness. Always extend loving thoughts to those around us. What you see in others is what you will see in yourself, and you'll reproduce that vibration in your immediate environment. You are attracting that which you are, or think you are. If you are attuning to the highest vision of your true self, how can you go wrong? There are also two words you need to eradicate from your vocabulary: *hate* and *try*. Hate, because you can't have hate as part of your mindset even if you are talking about the corned beef sandwich you had for lunch. Try, because if you say you will try something, it implies that you aren't going to do it now, only sometime in the future.

Learn to set a mental equivalent of gentleness and generosity and act with poise, grace, loving-kindness, ease, and serenity. You'll be surprised how little practice you will need until you permanently internalize those peaceful qualities within and find others possessing those qualities who are part of your everyday experience.

Practicing verbal harmlessness also applies to what you say about *you*. Nothing lowers your vibration quicker than self-criticism. Whatever you say about yourself applies to everyone because we're the same soul substance – and what you see in a mirror is what you will see in every person in your life. If I say *I* am weak, poor, or broke, I am saying *you* are too, because we are the same substance. Further, if I say I am stupid, I have just called the Divine stupid – not empowered thinking! By putting yourself down, you are conditioning your mind to believe it, which means you are focusing on lack in yourself. How can the infinite self lack? Become conscious of the spirit within you as your infinite supply. Know that you are composed of perfect soul material. Keep your affirmations in the present tense, be positive, stop using *hate* and *try*, stop self-criticism, and know that you are already wonderfully rich.

Start Today Because Today Is What Matters

Seeing an abundant world and drop-kicking faulty belief systems do take some practice. Having spent time at both ends of the financial spectrum over the years, I can say with a high degree of certainty that obstacles to our own success and abundance are inside either our heads or our souls. Both possibilities frighten us because they put responsibility for what we have in our lives, and for what we see demonstrated in the world, upon each of us, each individual.

Through my own business ventures and being a participant-observer in Tom's, I've made plenty of errors. I've had the wrong intentions, lost focus, didn't want to make clear choices. It's frustrating, and often painful, to accept that we are in charge of the program. Who wants to accept that strife or failure is created by our own hand? I think our first impulse is to retreat into a corner and let someone else participate, especially after we stumble. Hence we tend to block our own potential, and until we grudgingly admit this, it is much easier to blame our perceived inability to demonstrate an abundant life on something or someone else who stands in our light while we live in the shadows.

The world is a demonstration of what is inside our heads. We are here to create *exactly* what we hold in our consciousness. We *must* participate in this process – it's why we are here! Remember, part of our purpose is to express the Divine in physical form, but a little room for human error makes the experience more creative. It makes us more endearing. It's what makes human triumph so exhilarating. It permits us to evolve. We can get it right in our own personal lives first, then take it to a higher level and go for world change. What have we got to lose by changing our thoughts, other than changing our lives?

The keys to the castle are not the privileged life, luck, family or self-made money, majority or minority status, gender, or great looks. There's no secret door to open, nobody has been bootlegging a trade secret across enemy lines, an initiation rite does not take place at the abundance sorority to which only a select few are offered membership. The answer lies in how you construct your own mental equivalent, which is the beginning of an abundant life. The biggest breakthrough in your abundance mindset is to know you *can* create anything you want with as much prosperity as you can imagine. Go for it and demonstrate heaven on earth.

Consciously Create Your Day

Wake up with visions of prosperity and abundance. Unseat old,
negative programs when the impulse strikes! I hope you will find
the following affirmations helpful in changing faulty thinking.

Can't-Afford Mindset

*When I dwell on the idea of lack, I build a consciousness of lack
and it attracts more lack. Whatever I ask for, I receive, because
the natural state of the unlimited universe is to provide for me.
I now have a mindset of abundance because my source is unlimited! I am part of a universal order that provides an abundant
and inexhaustible supply. I see abundance reflected in all areas
of my life. My income and all things that are valuable to me are
prospering and growing bigger as I notice how much abundance
there is in the world.*

Lacking Abundance

*Because the world is a perfect gift, I already have everything. I
accept my gifts with joy. Every day I rise in a state of thankfulness
for all that exists, especially for the blessings in my life. I exist in
a state of peace and thankfulness for what I have, knowing that
the universe is working with me to manifest what I desire. I do not
believe in lack; I believe in prosperity, which is my natural state.*

Money Never Comes Easily

*I am grateful for every gift in my life. I am an open channel to
receiving all my goodness, no matter where it comes from. I am
now opening the door to an abundant and prosperous world, and
I step through with joy. I love being receptive to all good in my
life. I thank the universe for every gift that comes my way and
know I am always ready to receive my good from everywhere,
everything, and everyone.*

NOT ENOUGH MONEY

My prosperity is a reflection of my consciousness. Therefore the thoughts I hold in my mind are of abundance. There is an unlimited supply of money in the universe that is constantly increasing. I deserve to prosper. I release my old, limiting ideas about lack, because I no longer believe in lack. When others have more money than I do, it takes nothing away from me because there is enough for everyone.

For more affirmations, see my companion book, *The Women's Book of Empowerment: 323 Affirmations That Change Everyday Problems into Moments of Potential* (The Goddess Network Press, 2005). Available through any major online book retailer or at www.thegoddessnetwork.net.

Taking Spiritual Inventory:
Living with Abundance

Analyze

Where do our prosperity and abundance attitudes come from? Creating an abundant life is about mastering the process of thinking. Your abundance is not determined by outside conditions but is a manifestation of your beliefs about what is possible. Ask yourself:

* Was I raised in a family where I felt guilty about "having"? Did my family make me feel that having money or material things was bad? Did we diminish our prosperity consciousness because I was told that it was evil (or bad, snotty, selfish) to have means? Do I have negative past programming about money and success? Were my parents uncomfortable with money?

* Do I reward myself only when I lack what I want in my life? Do I reward myself only when I fail?

* Have I been afraid to be a success? Am I success-conscious or deprivation-conscious? Do I deserve to have what I want? Do I love the vision of enjoying what I want in life and feel joyful about a self-image of success?

* Do I believe that having takes something away from someone else? Do I believe in the concept of lack? Am I truly happy for others' success and prosperity, or do I believe that someone who "has" diminishes my present or future opportunities?

* Is the universe limited in its potential to provide for everyone? If I believe in a world with limits, then how can I realize my potential? Is spirit limited in what it can do? If not, what is limiting me, if I am a spark of the Divine?

* Is money the only tool to reach my potential?
* Am I in a constant state of awareness of who I am, which is spirit? If spirit is within, and spirit is unlimited, then I am unlimited in what I can do. Is that statement easy or difficult for me to accept? Why?
* Am I truly thankful, and do I regularly express thanks to the universe for the goodness I have received? When I ask for something and visualize it, do I thank in advance for what I am about to receive, knowing that I have already received it? Is it possible for me to believe I have received something, even though I do not see it immediately? Why or why not?
* Do I pay bills with a thankful heart? Do I pay with love and joy? Or do I pay with anger and resentment? Do I appreciate the ability I have to pay a bill?

Affirm

Hold a constant state of prosperity consciousness. Making room for more abundance in life is about clarity (knowing what you want) and interest (feeling deep emotion, for example, love, joy, happiness) when you visualize having what you want. Write your own affirmation that helps you feel that being abundant and prosperous is a joyful exchange between you and the universe.

_____

_____

_____

_____

_____

_____

_____

_____

_____

_____

_____

Write an affirmation that enlarges your idea of prosperity, and share the affirmation with someone. Know your supply is limitless and begin to recognize abundance in everything.

Walk the Talk

You will attract more abundance in your life with the right actions. Actions are symbolic and meaningful. Be generous: offer a gift in the form of compliment. Clean closets to make more room for opportunity in your life. If money is an expression of your nature and the divine, how can it change the way you act? How can you express your "money self"? List three activities that put a positive spin on your actions as a prosperous individual, whether you have money or not.

Another activity to try is a gratitude walk, which is a walking prayer and meditation. With every step you take, find a new way to appreciate and count your blessings. A gratitude walk is a way to demonstrate, or ritualize, thankfulness for your prosperity. Go to a peaceful place, preferably outdoors, and ask spirit to light your way through the day. Clear all thoughts from your mind except those of joy and gratitude. Dedicate your walk to a certain area of your life – work, family, your creative genius – and recognize your sacred path. With each series of steps, identify with the unlimited abundance of the universe.

Share the Spirit

Creating a new mental equivalent to attract abundance and prosperity in your life requires discipline. With clear intentions and a steady focus, you will manifest what you want. You've already experienced this in your life. What memories do you have of a past circumstance where you were very focused on getting what you want, and you received it? What do you remember about the experience of manifesting? Write down a new dream you have, and the mental equivalent you need to make it happen.

My Dream

_____

_____

_____

_____

_____

_____

_____

_____

_____

_____

My Mental Equivalent

_____

_____

_____

_____

_____

_____

_____

_____

_____

_____

_____

_____

_____

Now vocalize your dream. Share it with someone, describe it with great detail, and say why you believe your dream can come true.

I TAKE MY SPIRITUAL TRUTH
TO WORK EVERY DAY
AND DEMONSTRATE IT IN
EVERYTHING I DO.

Corporate Soul

Use Spirit and
Strength to
Guide Work Life

Bringing the Awakened Self to Work

The way I get through my day?
I pretend I am a great, big, powerful octopus.

– Belisha, daycare provider

Glancing at my business schedule alerts me to an undeniable fact: on some days, viewing work as a positive experience and as an expression of my true self is far more demanding than my job. Staying in a balanced, self-affirming mindset (and keeping everyone else there) through the ups and downs of generating abundance for an organization is what most leaders will agree is the one activity that takes the most effort – and the one that, with the clock always ticking, usually gets put on the back burner. We spend so much time managing complexity, massaging the team, forecasting the market, and focusing on the goal that we lose sight of developing our soul, the entire reason we're participating in the workforce in the first place. Who has time to reflect on what work *means?* And if we figure out how our chosen occupation fits into our own unique soul story, how can we bring a sense of spiritual purpose to our organizations, as either employees or leaders?

Articulating a sense of soulfulness and contributing to the greater good have nothing to do with gender, as everyone is capable of bringing their authentic self to the office. However, having had a job since I was thirteen years old has entitled me to make a few specific observations about women in the workforce. The first is that we've denied the feminine side of ourselves for too long: we do not realize that the qualities we inherit as women are as sacred and important as the men in our lives. We can conceptualize ourselves as both male and female spirit, both God and Goddess, equally divine and beloved. The feminine side of God has been diminished for so long that we've come to believe we are something less important, because we can't see ourselves in images of God. And our failure to acknowledge ourselves as sparks of that collective essence, both Mother and Father God, can make us feel unworthy and flawed. It translates into low self-esteem, because we believe our true self is less important. It permeates relationships, and before we know it, we have developed an unworthy state of mind, and then begin to create that in our immediate experience. In the workplace, it has affected our overall confidence level when we compare ourselves with men doing the same type of jobs.

Since Henry Mintzberg's observations in his 1973 diary studies of executives, management styles have drastically changed. Old ways, as well as the old boys' network, have steadily been dismantled in favor of organizational structures that encompass more female-friendly policies and ideas, with the idea of empowering the female through equal opportunity and culture change. Throughout this process, women stumbled on the rocky road to empowerment, adapting to public and private realms still encumbered by unspoken, old-fashioned and traditionally bureaucratic parameters. Women slid into the workforce in a fairly male-dominated environment and believed they needed to adapt. They thought that by managing exactly like men, they would attract power.

But now, as a body of research is developing, we're learning that we were barking up the wrong tree. Our own woman culture, our entire system of shared meaning and knowledge, is intact. After twenty years we have learned that self-power or empowerment does not happen by riding on the top of the hierarchical heap as a pseudo-man. It doesn't even come from manpower disguised as womanpower. It comes from a sense of appreciating and knowing at the deepest level possible that we are truly worthy because we are an image of the highest power that exists. We are beginning to realize that what constitutes our beingness is as divine as what constitutes a man's, because we are the same soul substance.

Although we love God, and we *are* God, we are also the Goddess. And we're beginning to love ourselves for who we are, which includes *both* aspects of a divine equation, because self-love is about demonstrating that which is within, our spiritual power. Female qualities and values that are precipitated from this spiritual composite will someday be demonstrated at the highest levels of organizations with great success. However, for now it seems we must first be more comfortable in our own skin and acknowledge at last that what we contribute has tremendous significance, to society as well as to the bottom line.

> Sure, I'd love to work for Ben & Jerry's or the Body Shop. Anything to get in a more woman-affirming office ... I wish I could find places that make me feel like I'm tuned into a higher purpose.
>
> *Kelly, corporate jet dispatcher*

My second observation about women in the workforce is that once we define and embrace the feminine side of our spiritual composite, we will re-embrace the masculine principle in a more balanced fashion. The result will be the institution of a set of values that correspond to who we are and what we do well. If we allow it, our feminine side will begin to reconceptualize leadership roles that include affirming, dynamic views of our self-development process. Work will be viewed as a unique service to the larger community. This will be done through new policies we set, reflected in our decision styles, and by outlining the long-term objectives of what our organizations need to accomplish in order to make sense from the *act* of working.

At a very deep level, the glorious aspects that make up the yin side of us are our core competency – and we're seeing evidence that harnessing those energies in ways that assist one another in our spiritual evolution can make us better in our work. In the future, knowing how we co-create with spirit will become the mission and vision for organizations that will finally permit everyone, not just women, to fabricate meaning from doing.

The Changing Workplace

I remember with amusement the corporate uniforms of the Eighties – tailored man's suits in female-friendly colors with gigantic shoulder pads – that made us feel important by representing the enormous burdens we thought we could carry. Women en masse rose to the challenge of navigating within the boardroom, billiard room, ballroom, and bedroom – sometimes all in the same day. We got over our sensitivity, learned how to smoke cigars, strapped babies on our backs, and forged ahead with night school MBAs. Because we shared work experiences with men who occupied most positions of authority in American institutions, it was natural to follow the rules of the dominant culture in order to succeed. We adopted male leadership styles and performance criteria, recognizing the importance of squash and golf.

Then women hit a long drive that translated twenty years later into astounding statistics: in 2000, nearly 46 percent of the labor force was female, and the proportion is climbing. The face of the workforce became completely different, and along with technology and the influence of the global economy, the workplace metamorphosed into a fundamentally different environment. Companies had to redesign the skill sets needed to manage complexity. Women exercised power differently, not less effectively, and men paid attention to how women focused on collaborative processes, resulting in profitable outcomes. Female work

> I love that more of us are managers and presidents. What scares me is we might have to keep doing things around here the same way.
>
> *Debra, human resource coordinator for a furniture manufacturer*

culture expanded and women asked to be included. Work began to fit the woman and not the other way around.

The changing workplace is experienced by everyone, and we see a distinctly different female work style emerging. Women focus more energy on strengthening relationships, are concerned about the wider needs of their community, don't care as much as men about the workings of a hierarchy, and certainly see themselves as the center of the web. Is it any wonder? When I first read the research on female-led organizations, describing how women managers are redefining their workplaces with these values in dramatically successful ways, it occurred to me that we are simply rediscovering what we already know: women are beginning to honor their own spiritual composite by no longer needing to see themselves within the corset of old male management structures and philosophies that held them captive for so long. They are transferring what they do well into tangible results, in the form of high profits and customer satisfaction. They are beginning to harness their own capabilities, finding a voice that is true to their calling. And here's the exciting part: today's women have the capacity to transform the world by making wider changes because they are assuming roles of substantial authority.

As researchers are tackling the subject of women in the workforce, some interesting results are taking shape: feminine leadership styles and values as well as the ancient women's way of knowing (our intuitive side) are positive features finally being revived in a new management equation: a woman's way of doing things equals profitable organizations with happier employees. Women believe that people are more productive when they *feel* good about themselves. Among our inventory of assets: a focus on unity, relatedness, earth, compassion, and intuition. A celebration is in order – our emotional side is finally recognized as a good thing.

Women have *always* viewed themselves as the center of the web, as they are the conduits for life and generally have a deep, spiritual connection to it, not just through children and families but in all organic matter, because we know what it feels like to generate and facilitate the life-giving principle. We are life-givers because there is female in *everything*. And when life itself is abused in our business practices, the environment, relationships, children, or even pets, we feel it down to the depths of our soul. We are committed to keeping it going in all venues because that's been our job since the beginning. Yes, there's a reason we blubber at movies. We're the sensitive, self-appointed caretakers of the universe and the new community glue for organizations.

A New (and Old) Women's Workplace Philosophy

Everyone is born with a basic impulse to illuminate the world with unique capabilities. Our true occupation is to remember our spirit, and to re-embrace who we are at the deepest level possible and bring it on, regularly refueling as we go. The challenge on the horizon is to fuse spirit into organizational life as an expression of our divine essence, and allow work to become a more complete expression of who we are.

Women already own an everyday spirituality, a philosophy developed through the art of living and common sense and not necessarily as a function of dogma. Some rely on religion, of course, along with reflection, prayer, and consulting the higher powers. But when it

> Growing up, I don't think I heard one thing in school about history from a woman's perspective. We revisit all the other atrocities in major wars in detail, but so little is mentioned about the extermination of women, such as in the witch burnings and in the middle ages. If [historians] don't explain the misperception people had about Pagan religion, everyone will continue to think those acts were justified.
>
> *Candice, women's clothing salesperson, practicing Pagan*

comes to the workforce, it's a tentative expression for either group, partly because spiritual beliefs must be compartmentalized when creating work policies, in our conversations with our employers, or in public educational environments. This necessary separation permits us to enjoy the diversity and freedom of this society, but as a result, it has created a big divide between us and our source. For women, a lack of female imagery expands the degree of separation, in that mainstream religion makes little reference to female deity and speaks a god-language created by men. The result is even more distance from our source because we don't recognize the Divine in our mirrors and haven't for a very long time.

So much of the sacred literature of many wisdom traditions, considered to be the word of a loving and perfect male creator, has sent negative signals, beginning with creation myths. Eve's sin and punishment were used to explain the right of men to subjugate and oppress women, locking them into inferior roles for centuries. God's word offered divine proof that woman could not be whole unto herself: only man could, because he was made in the image of a male creator. Hopefully, today's woman (and also man) has got past some of these writings, which have made independent females throughout history – intellectuals, healers, and teachers – the recipients of violence in the name of religion. Inquisitions and witch hunts based in fear of the female principle have not only diminished women's self-image but destabilized society, in the form of abusive and unbalanced marriages. Barring women from property ownership rights, the ability to vote, or participation in religious rites diminished their contributions, further preventing them from seeing themselves as a valuable societal and economic resource.

Our contemporary common sense tells us that women are not meant to be silent, obedient models of a passive principle; they are pure energy in the flesh, a symbol of the cycle of life, empowered by individual purpose. Women facilitate the web of life through many channels of power and wisdom. They are among the most authoritative and powerful vehicles of transformation through which community happens. They are capable of transferring this power to others to do the same, with great passion, as spiritual or business leaders in any organizational setting, including the family. Our proven track record needs to be told again when we lose sight of the big picture.

Women experience even more lack of connectivity to spirit in the current workplace environment because it retains remnants of an old, unbalanced organizational structure and still values old male virtues such as autonomy, conquest, and control. In order to compete, women have adapted well in the rule department – thank goodness, or we'd still be waiting for the suffragettes. But it is apparent that what is still missing in organizational metaphors is a mirror reflection of both feminine and masculine aspects of divinity, a source of inspiration that encourages positive, power-sharing, and co-affirming relationships. A balanced self-image and lifestyle is always drawn from images of a loving and balanced God. It is the fundamental basis of success, helping us to make sense of life and of ourselves. Without this, we will continue to misunderstand the consequences of culture and politics, and continue to facilitate an unspoken undercurrent of inequality in the guise of a round table.

Because so little has been written on how women make the link between spirit, values, and work, we can only refer to what appears to be the current growing appreciation of feminine values illustrated by the marketplace, the media, and educational programs for women and teen girls. Websites are springing up whose sole purpose is to point out negative advertising by companies that cheapen female imagery into objectified love vessels. Loving the body as sacred, learning to view life as an integrated whole, celebrating emotion, and balancing logic with intuition do make a better world. While society fine-tunes a collective man/woman

value set, women can begin to be champions of change, as new venues develop
in which we can have a voice over such
matters.

In the business sector, the twenty-
first-century equivalent of the quilting
bee is the leadership and executive seminar designed to increase awareness of
female work culture and helping to rede-
fine traditional workplace values. These
programs now equip leaders with understanding of how to connect their own
personal missions with that of the organization, so that a combined spirit and
energy of leaders can align with corporate insights. Yet outside
these seminars, in hallways, homes, and women's luncheons,
is the real dialogue: what women *believe in* is contradictory to
what they *experience* in their workplace, causing self-conflict and
stress. If we're all supposed to bring our entire selves to work,
doesn't that mean our philosophy and spirituality come along for
the ride? After all, we've been raised to believe that our beliefs are
the foundation for our communities. Even as women move into
powerful positions in the world economy, could this be why they
don't *feel* empowered?

We already know we must bring our divine essence to work,
our entire selves, in order to be truly happy and productive and
feel esteemed. But women are beginning to question the basis of
their wisdom traditions and wonder why they have accepted self-
images that do not fully allow them to feel empowered at work
and at home. Is there only a divine Father and no Mother? And in
a diverse global society, is there only one true path to Him? With
all the modern evidence of a fully competent and self-sufficient
female population, why aren't we whole unto ourselves? Has reli-

gion held everyone back from creating a mental equivalent of balance and equal empowerment?

Mothers are wondering why they are raising daughters to think outside the box but still within artfully limited image-parameters. And daughters are beginning to lift the veil to see what's underneath. While they are told they have unlimited opportunities in school and the workplace, their religions may contradict their strong self-image by exiling any sort of feminine power that comes from within. If women believe that Adam was created first and Eve second, that Adam was deceived by Eve and consequently the entire human race fell out of paradise and into sin, how can modern women possibly feel good about their gender? How can they hold their own in a competitive organizational arena, or even in relationships and in communities? Whether these ideas are seen as historical representations of the imaginings of our Hebrew ancestors or taken as the literal truth, women's search for their own sense of value must move away from shame and sin and instead toward reclaiming their original goodness.

For women to succeed in any venue, they need to be more in tune with themselves as spiritual beings, then move into a vision of a balanced idea of divinity. The residual effect will be the translation of *what female is* into a set of workplace values. True empowerment comes first from within, because it is based upon the knowledge that we are our true self.

At the most abstract level, our God-source is a pretty hard concept to articulate into a set of principles we can post on our lunchroom walls. How can we relate to a higher power that works for everyone? Since we are sparks of the Divine, we are also composed of both He and She principles called intellect and emotion, two essential elements of a spiritual equation that defines who we are. Thus far, we haven't given ourselves permission to fuse logic and feeling in our self-image, let alone in the workplace.

When we express both ideas in our spirituality, it will

naturally translate into everyday behaviors, both inside and outside the office. We'll wind up loving one another with greater passion and begin to arrive at new levels of gratitude for the opposite sex, in any place we happen to be together. Our culture will become one of appreciation for the way we do things differently; it will encompass deeper levels of understanding of that which binds us together, both men and women, who are capturing the same essence albeit differently by gender. And once we understand how that idea translates into work behaviors, we can make room for new styles of leadership, and consequently new organizations, with plenty of soul.

Intellect (He) and Emotion (She)

The concept of a higher power having dual aspects has been offered by numerous wisdom traditions, from the texts of Aurobindo on the sacred marriage, to the yin and yang, the fusion between two distinct spiritual counterparts. For thousands of years, Hindus, Buddhists, and Christians have explored through written and musical tradition the meaning of the masculine and feminine principles as a harmonious relationship of opposites. Many traditions refer to a unified God-principle, the concept of the sacred marriage, or an integrated divinity comprising dual characteristics. Together, they constitute the concept of the Divine as a totality.

It becomes easier to recognize the Divine in ourselves in terms we can relate to, as evidenced by the multitude of allegories, myths, scriptures, and poems passed down on the subject that help us assign meaning to abstract concepts. For example, the sacred marriage has been interpreted as a symbol of mystical unity. In the Gospel of Thomas, another of the Gnostic gospels, Jesus explains: "When you make the two one, and when you make the outside like the inside, and the above like the below, and when you make the male and the female one and the same, so that the male be not male nor the female female then will you enter the kingdom."

The kingdom is the spiritual awareness of a mystical union of two concepts: the masculine and feminine principles of God, both Father and Mother, a union between the God-man and the Goddess, a spiritual marriage of the bridegroom and the bride. The sacred marriage refers to the intertwined principles of intellect and emotion. It is a synthesis of the masculine and feminine principles in a conscious state, or in our bodily awareness, but also *before* such consciousness was achieved, when intellect and emotion existed as the source, or the kingdom, where no delineation is made between dual characteristics. The source is an eternal union of interdependent opposites, a polarity, a symbol of female and male who are bound by an equally important eternal rhythm. One cannot exist without the other, and one is no less important than the other.

How Do We Imagine Intellect and Emotion?

Imagine the Divine, comprising both the masculine and the feminine consciousnesses, called intellect and emotion. Intellect represents the Father, the masculine part of our nature, and all static knowledge, in the form of pure thought. He has often been referred to as "the immovable mover," a life force holding everything constant, the entire universe and beyond. He consists of every thought in its infinite complexity. Religious doctrine has often portrayed the He portion of God as transcendent, a perfection we rise to meet.

Emotion represents the creative energy aspect of ourselves, the Mother, and the feminine part of our nature. Imagine emotion as the impulse, the energy, a life force giving birth to intellect. She demonstrates or manifests knowledge and brings it into being or physical form. She has often been referred to as the Great Mother, the divine feminine principle, or the Great Goddess who provides the hands-on life-learning experience on earth.

The feminine principle is what provides the temporary illusion that we are separated from spirit, because in order to experience life, we must separate part of ourselves from our source to be in a body. Emotion, or female principle, generates the soul experience. In other words, it is through *her* energy that He is realized, because She allows Him to realize his beingness. She has been referred to as immanent, an instrument of thought providing form that enables thought to move and experience. For us to evolve, our divine mother has given us an opportunity to be here and now, not in some other dimension where we might be at a later date. It says a lot about the sacredness of the human experience.

Both elements of God-Father-He/Goddess-Mother-She are completely interdependent and equal. *Intellect is defined by emotion.* An idea is dependent upon experience to give it full meaning. You can have pure thought (intellect), but if there is no experience of that thought, there is nothing to give it definition. For example, if I create an intellectual idea such as love, I know what love is, what it does, and its importance. But without the *experience* of the love idea, there can be no true knowingness of love; it must be demonstrated, or manifested, to experience all the ways we can know love.

Emotion is also defined by intellect. You cannot have emotion, or experience, without a thought pattern behind it. We can't build ships without blueprints! So She represents the emotion or energy required to do that. She, the Mother, is the feminine portion of this model and represents the tangible aspects of life, the choices we have in making knowledge manifest. This process is what facilitates our soul development: the ability to go beyond the idea *through* physical experience and, in the process, to demonstrate spirit, or God-heaven, on earth.

Through many wisdom traditions, we see a variety of metaphors and images that express a harmonious interdependency of complementary spiritual and human realities. They are present within every individual. Exploring these boundaries of consciousness and questioning the relationship between the fundamental ideas of independence and community are among our most basic impulses in the human condition.

Mother/Feminine	Father/Masculine
✿ Heart	✿ Mind
✿ Emotion	✿ Intellect
✿ Being	✿ Thinking
✿ Intuition	✿ Reason/logic/analysis
✿ Community	✿ Hierarchy
✿ Relatedness/unity/ complementarity	✿ Individualization/ differentiation
✿ Spontaneity/ unencumberedness	✿ Planning
✿ Earth	✿ Sky
✿ Object	✿ Subject
✿ The embodiment of intelligence	✿ The blueprint
✿ The embodiment of what is	✿ What is
✿ Night and moon	✿ Day and sun
✿ Speech	✿ Word
✿ Shared power	✿ Domination
✿ Action	✿ Static knowledge
✿ Chaos	✿ Order
✿ Multiplicity	✿ Linearity
✿ Belonging	✿ Separateness

The dynamic interaction of intellect and emotion expresses an important truth about the cosmos. We live in an environment of balance seeking polarities. We have male and female, light and dark, left and right, giving and receiving, day and night. It's evident everywhere: all species want to define one another by fitting together. Even our internal circuitry reflects a polarity of positive and negative. We are living examples of our divine nature in the form of gender polarity. And bringing both together in conscious communion with each other, as a single, unified reality, will reestablish balance in our world.

UNITY OF INTELLECT AND EMOTION

The Chinese characterize the totality of God (the Tao or the Dao) not as a static and transcendent being but as unity, experienced in the manifest as well as the unmanifest world. In their view, God is without beginning or end, a "cosmic wholeness" or "primal simplicity," and has no definition. In its most abstract form, God is source, which is what exists before God becomes the created. When spirit is created, or shows itself in forms, it can be defined, but not until then.

> I love Shakti, she is so powerful. She doesn't take anything away from her male spiritual counterpart, she just makes him better.
>
> *Shamala, professor of architectural design*

In its primal state, or in the abstract, God is beyond the confines of human language, beyond even the terms of intellect and emotion.

This principle of Dao, or an image of the godhead, is akin to what the Gnostics called the divine essence. In their view, God does not create. The divine essence emanates, or comes forth, from an unmanifested state into the manifest, in two distinctive patterns in a simultaneous, dynamic process. The act of emanation makes it possible to have further, more specific creation. It is an interaction between the undefined and creative energy, both of which constitute God. Translation: God's ability to emanate produced us in the flesh, courtesy of the Mother. The She principle defines the totality of God.

In the Indian tradition, the Rig-Veda describes Shakti as the embodiment of power and Shiva as inert. Shakti is the manifestation of energy characterized as female. Shiva, the Absolute, is thought to represent intellect, and is able to express himself in creation only *through* her. Without her, and her ability to transform his intellect, he remains inert and inactive – the immovable mover. While Shiva is able to intellectually create, he cannot come forth from an unmanifested state into the manifest, nor can he demonstrate his intellect unless united with Shakti. The unity is one of harmonious interdependence. From this perspective, God captures dual features. Intellect is demonstrated by experience, or emotion, which is the primal impulse that sets intellect, or the masculine principle, into definition. Through both principles, we are fully expressed.

Before we interpret this as a license to kick the men in our life off the couch and issue a mandate to pick up their socks, we should recognize that in the big picture, we can attain perfection if we live in accordance with both principles – the key to a balanced life. The active principle is what completes him, and the static principle is what completes her, allowing them both to achieve perfection. The two principles complete each other. For men and women of today, it means that life on earth is a sacred gift. It means our emotions are necessary to our evolution, as well as our choices and our entire lives on earth. We *need* female in order to succeed here and now, not at some moment in the future or in the afterlife. And we need our divine mother because She is part of us, completely necessary for the entire human race to evolve. Without the female principle, it doesn't happen. Among empowering thoughts, it doesn't get any more powerful than that.

Sky God, Earth Mother: A Little Ancient History

Clearly, for everyone to succeed, we must question why the female is still so underrated and underrepresented, especially as deity. What is so hard to accept about the divinity of the feminine? And why does so much negative imagery still exist in our religious literature? How on earth (and heaven) did we get to where we are today?

Society does take a great deal of direction from messages we receive from spirituality and religion, in spite of efforts to segregate the two. The exclusion of the feminine principle, and the consequent diminishment of the importance of women, arose partly from the ascendance of a monotheistic male god, itself a result of the rise of patriarchy. In the history of religion, the shift to a male-dominated patriarchal culture, with male values, happened around 4,000 years ago, before the ancient Hebrews. In a conversion to a monotheistic culture, one male universal god unseated goddess religion in order to rule the roost. This continued as late as the conversion of the Roman emperor Constantine in 320 C.E. and his imposition of Christianity as a state religion.

Men and women's ideas of deity have differed for thousands of years; numerous scholarly texts shed light on how our society has arrived at such different concepts of what women (and men) value. A long time ago, the Goddess was the big kahuna, the queen of the universe. People related to their earthbound existence by imagining that they lived within her vast womb, their lives a symbol for the birth, death, and rebirth seen in nature.

Goddess religion flourished for thousands of years before the advent of Christianity, Judaism, and Islam. The Goddess, a female image of a divine being, had been a model for men's and women's natures, especially for women, as the Goddess provided the main spiritual sustenance and a way to reflect on cultural values that made sense. The She-God was portrayed as Isis, Innana, Diana of Ephesus, Kuan Yin, Aphrodite, Demeter, and many other goddesses, as manifestations of the feminine principle. However, the takeover and subsequent obliteration of matrilineal cultures (where inheritance and line of descent were traced through the mother) meant that the image of the Goddess was divorced from divinity, reformulated, or reduced in significance, because it threatened a new social order.

> After I read *The Da Vinci Code*, something just made sense inside of me. Now, I see the mother principle everywhere. I feel like I have to catch up on something I missed.
>
> *Meaghan, orthodontic assistant*

Scholars have suggested that the emergence of male-dominated religions – originally designed to extinguish the female principle, female sexual autonomy, and matrilineal descent – permitted men to be the primary messengers of holy word through ritual and to assume property control and ownership of women. These attitudes still permeate our home and work lives, as the generations that accepted such church-inspired precepts are not that far removed from us.

There's a flavorful and amazing documented history of the emergence of the church and its role in usurping the property rights (land ownership) of women. With the ascent of the new state religion, those who revered the Great Goddess in ritual and prayer soon became obsolete, even a target of genocide. Some remnants of Her remain in the form of old goddess temples (many churches are built upon such sacred sites), and fortunately we still have Mary. It is interesting to imagine how very different today's world would be, not just in our religious diversity but in male-female relationships and our families, attitudes, and organizational structures, if we had assimilated positive and powerful ideas about women, who were never meant to be less a reflection of a divine image than men.

Accumulating historical and archaeological evidence has

revealed that societies dedicated to a female deity were entirely different from our own. The Goddess was not so much heaven-centered and transcendent but earth-centered and immanent. Through philosophy and ritual, She has persisted over the last 30,000 years. In her gradual gender change from Goddess to God, She's gone through a number of transitions. Once an image of supreme deity all on her own, She has undergone a shift to become one male supreme being who orders men to do his bidding. Over time, the change empowered men and sent women scurrying for cover. The biggest factor influencing our modern world might be that our very essence, originally a total image of an infinite creator, now favors the male part of the equation. And women have still not been able to unseat the fundamental inequities, evident in all facets of male-female relationships, both in the boardroom and at home.

Although there's been an apparent resurgence of goddess religion in the past twenty years, it is difficult to predict the future of the temple of Isis. Would a return to goddess religion shift the balance back to where it should be, empowering the women of the world while the men have their own brand of spirituality? I think it is too late, and a better scenario is to revisit the conceptual foundation of what He and She mean, as equal partners in creation. Saviors, prophets, and mystics aside, we still have not dealt with positive God imagery. We haven't made any room for She, and women as a unique subset of Her. We haven't even made room for men as a unique subset of Her. We've got a long way to go to institute real change.

THE WARRIOR SPIRIT

The writing and assembly of the Christian Bible was influenced by political considerations, and Judeo-Christian theologies in turn have formulated today's idea of the warrior. The warrior spirit takes some of its inspiration from the concept of the sky-god and draws upon monotheism, whose focus was on domination and logic without enough compassion. Male-dominated cultures had their own male values, centered on the warrior. From almighty Zeus, who was reputed to have given birth to his daughter Athena through the top of his head, and a host of other mighty combatants throughout folklore and mythology, we've kept the

> In our company, we are still talking about "eat or be eaten." It's a jungle out there. I know because I work in one.
>
> *Angela, stockbroker*

warrior spirit alive in our culture. Still championed in Monday-night football, it is about the courageous, conquering hero whose soul work involves capturing the booty, hopefully for the benefit of community survival. We've adopted the warrior spirit in the business world too, where it has been channeled into organizational models in the form of control, warlike metaphors such as "kill or be killed," and hierarchical communication structures.

Currently, our insightful management gurus force our attention to the changes demanded by the customer and attune us to the demands of innovation, but they haven't been able to fully channel our creative energy with any awareness of the partnership of our souls. Corporate spirituality is the new frontier of managing change and morality – it's the new religion laden with all the best of what we've conjured up as a human race: universal values of love, generosity, gratitude, and ethics. But we've been dancing around the real issue too long already. We need to reinvent work culture not only with vision and authenticity, humility, and forgiveness, but with true partnership that we understand and deploy at a deeply spiritual level. Our corporate message needs to revisit our multiplicity and the value of the feminine impulse as an emanation of the unifying force of love. We can't all be on a singular path to transcend to the Father, either directly or through one or more popular saviors. The path to love is also through the Mother aspect of God, in the here and now, and our immanent existence is also sacred. *She in us* is very much part of a balanced process of self-development.

To make real change in organizations, our religious and cultural undercurrent needs to adjust, because old imagery provides a philosophical and unspoken foundation of our self-image, affecting the way we relate to one another. It influences our marriages and relationships, how we choose our careers, and how we do business. After a revival of the feminine principle, women will begin to realize that it's OK to express our complete, woman-affirming self at work. Men will rely more on their feminine side, both sexes will harness their complete selves. Then everyone will begin to drive the point home that organizational life will be much more robust with the feminine spirit leading the pack – but alongside the warrior.

For we cannot operate solely with the guidance of the Goddess: in marketplace reality, the warrior spirit *must* exist in order for us to compete. For leaders, it takes a lot of carefully drafted inspiration to convince people to rise to a challenge through collaboration and good tactics. Without some element of the warrior, people feel they aren't working toward a goal. The good part of the warrior spirit, which both men and women have learned to internalize and demonstrate in their work, is the courage to rise up when faced with overwhelming odds and focus on the task at hand with a relentless charge. The warrior spirit mobilizes the strongest of the troops to the front lines to fight for survival, or to forge ahead when competing for vendor contracts or defending lawsuits. For those of us who have been in sales, grabbing a sword is something we do before we even put on our morning pantyhose. And retreating means we're out of a job and, worse, our community (business and families) can't survive. Even though there have been plenty of amazons and other female warriors, men have mostly led this charge and kept channeling this spirit into a set of values we've come to take as articles of faith. Women fundamentally have a different set of values. Why?

WARRIOR VALUES, GODDESS VALUES

A plausible theory is that we've nurtured ourselves in the domestic realm for so long that what we bring from home into the workplace is deeply ingrained in our skill set. Our concern for maintaining relationships and meeting human needs stems from staying behind while our tribes were protected by the strongest adult males. Sally Helgesen, author of *The Female Advantage*, refers to fearlessness, aggression, the ability to conceptualize the other as the enemy, and the fierce need to prove oneself in contests as "warrior values." Of course, these values cultivated and mobilized our heroes and permitted society's survival.

No need to apologize for our human evolution, but it seems that many places we work haven't been able to let this imagery go. Employee reward systems produce champions yet treat customers like coveted prizes, until the warrior gets weary of them and moves to greener pastures. We've learned to do business like satraps, squashing the competition with a lot of muscle and not enough wisdom and love. Business and other contemporary work environments do not have to be scenes of war or bloody battles to the death. I've been on the receiving end of this emotionally draining metaphor, and it is difficult to sustain. The competition is not the enemy; it exists merely to make the work process more interesting through what we hope to be civilized conflict in the pursuit of a common goal.

> Thank God I retired when I could. I was so weary of big-company politics.
>
> *Tammi, training coordinator for a Big Three automaker*

Because of educational opportunities, high divorce rates, and economic pressures, women have chosen the front lines and, out of necessity, adopted warrior values. Our sisters who broke new ground back in the Sixties put on the morning battle gear to slay the lions for the sake of their families; they built up the troops only to find themselves losing their positions to a bunch of nonsense like hierarchical control and rigidly defined work roles. The signs of internal conflict began to show. The fallout, in the form of high stress and early burnout, has been evidence of the disconnect with our basic need to express our essence.

The battle is taking a toll on our hearts because we naturally fight the impulse to fight. What we really want to do is build communities and environments that *nurture* our own sense of completion in creative, mentally challenging, efficient, and profitable ways that do not compromise the human race. Unsurprisingly, the stats show that women have been spending a lot of career time in human resource positions, support and administration, and highly specialized professions that deploy direct means of communication and nurturing – skill sets that are now spilling over into manning departmental and organizational helms. But we've already been inundated with too many management principles about how to achieve more success and be happier, so let's revisit the basics. Work, in fact, needs to be an extension of how we run the home base. A work culture that includes women has to include the sensible values of the female.

To develop our own set of values, fueled with a lot of feminine power, we can refer to some of the most primitive and abstract imagery of the Goddess: we are both weavers and the web, we are the givers of life. We're not spears – linear, pointed, and direct. We are the energy circles, the center of everything, and we can reconceptualize ourselves as a circle of influence. We're wombs who hold the power of creative ideas that better the world. While everyone collectively continues to flatten organizations and redesign the work environment to accommodate both wombs and spears, we'll evolve together and put our feminine side to the test. We don't want to think like men, compete like men, and manage organizations like men. We want to compete on our own terms, as multi-taskers directing traffic at the center of the circle, having both warrior and nurturing qualities. And as we come back to ourselves in the end, we might discover how much power we have to harness the female capacity to change the world.

INTELLECT AND EMOTION, INC.: A BETTER ORGANIZATION

In order to move toward a workplace with a lot of corporate soul, we must know our authentic selves at a very deep level but also understand the big picture. Employers and employees alike are enrolled in soul development school, no matter where they are within the organizational strata. The complexity of how we bring our wisdom and spiritual insight to our jobs and working relationships must be precipitated from spiritual essence, the one great equalizer that ties us to the real world. Our companies *are* an extension of our spiritual value set. Let's make the work environment something that works for everyone, so we can finally join together for a common purpose and experience some personal growth.

> Maybe some places are interested in the total person – we're not just cogs in a machine. It's definitely changing, but I don't think so for smaller businesses. We would never talk about spirit in the workplace.
>
> *Micky, baker*

At the most abstract level of interpretation, the organizational metaphor we need for our world today is that of God and Goddess. When we achieve balance between the two sides that constitute our image (intellect and emotion), we *become* that metaphor by expressing both aspects through the act of living and working. Many leaders have recognized that body, mind, and spirit in balance are elements of our totality, and the way we *think* of ourselves determines our world and the balance of power. The truth is that as long as we're out of balance as spiritual individuals, our politics, relationships, and workplaces will continue to be out of balance.

In order to make change in the world, we simply need to give more attention to one side of our spiritual equation. Let's set aside more space for our feminine side and merge our He and She furniture. Although the concepts of love and the Divine are universal and gender-free, we still must see ourselves in the Divine to see those ideas in the world we create. To bring a balanced image of God and self into our work, and into every aspect of our daily lives, we must operate with a foothold in each concept, yielding a collective set of values based on mutual respect.

Affirming the Best in You and Your Workplace

Without understanding a value base and the nature of the strength we draw on, it's nearly impossible to ride the worst of the workforce bumps. If we're going to improve the quality of life, we've got to first give up the excessive use of the warrior force and make some room for the Goddess. A winner-or-loser mindset may work for the championship series but is no longer a good metaphor for navigating through workplace strife. Do you recognize any of the following negative thought patterns about work and career, stemming from unbalanced warrior values?

Kill or be killed. Business is war.

This is my territory to defend. Winning is everything.

Only the fastest one to the finish line will win.

At all costs, we've got to get this account.

We've got to do whatever it takes to bring home the bacon.

I've worked hard to get to the top of the heap, and I will do whatever it takes to stay there.

I need to be in charge to be successful. Nobody can do it like me.

I am the job. I am nothing without this job.

We also bring many self-defeating thoughts to the conference table, ones that do not resonate with a balanced self-image. Negative thinking stems from a lack of God-self empowerment. You may recognize these in yourself or others.

I can do only one thing. If I can't do that, I can't do anything else.

I can't admit I made a mistake; it would make me weaker.

There's no room for emotions. Numbers are logical, feelings are illogical.

Making money is all that matters. I'm defined by my salary.

Why should I think outside the box? Nobody pays me to do that. That's someone else's job.

My self-worth is dependent upon how many sales I generate.

This company is draining the life out of me.

I can't stand my boss. Why should I work so hard?

Only the people at the top get what they want. They do it at my expense.

I don't matter in this large organization.

I'm not going to be on the planet forever, so why should I worry what I do to the earth?

Nobody notices my talents.

I'll just be a little cog in the big machine.

Work stinks.

I'm just doing my time until I retire (or quit).

Why should I work smarter or learn? I should just be paid for what I know right now.

I don't have to keep on learning to keep my job.

I'm not in charge of my own success - it's someone else's responsibility.

I'm not capable of seeing the big picture. Having a vision is someone else's job.

Management takes everything and I get nothing.

It's everyone else's fault I was let go.

I don't make a difference around here.

I'm not in charge of my financial destiny.

I've been here twenty years. I've earned a place because I did my time.

I deserve to be taken care of.

Customers are there to be used. We need their money.

It is "buyer beware" - let it be their problem.

I shouldn't have to disclose what I do in my job. It's my domain.

Overall, we can override negative thinking through the lens of intellect and emotion - and we can help guide others to success when we view work as an extension of an entire culture, not a zero-sum game.

Before we enter the workforce, we ought to realize that a lifetime spent building portfolios as an expression of our abilities will not offer us any larger sense of completion unless it is accompanied by the following knowledge: the process of self-expression is meant to deploy our sense of connection to a spiritual power. To be happy in all aspects of our life, whether our work is at a Fortune 500 company or at home with the kids, we must learn to translate the Divine through the work we do.

Our workplace is self-development school, a testing ground for the ideas we treasure. But we need to learn how to balance what we do well with doing the right thing for others, in ways that create rewards for *everyone*. Although our jobs may be flavored with our own individual talent and sense of humor, perfecting the soul is a career objective. We must be in tune with both our intellect and our emotions in order to work successfully with others. Our muse is a balanced image of divinity. In this way, we learn to step outside of ourselves and be a witness to our own experience.

Remember, you are fortunate to have the opportunity to join hands with others. The act of that alone is a sacred expression. When we manage people and problems facing our culture in the image of God/Goddess, and with great patience, love, and compassion, the rewards are great. That is why we affirm, especially during times when we believe we have failed miserably and our confidence is shaken:

> I really do love serving other people, at all ages and situations they have in life. It makes me want to get up in the morning.
>
> *Adele, charity fundraiser*

I am an expression of that which is within me. I am my soul substance, embracing both intellect and emotion, which seek expression through me. My circumstances are temporary but offer me a sacred learning experience and an opportunity to grow my soul. My presence is needed every day and in every way. When I think of myself as He and She, I attract that which seeks expression through me, which is the power of both Mother and Father God. I am empowered by my own divinity, my true self, which brings balance to my work situation.

Consciously Create Your Day

Draw strength from a balanced image of the Divine and know that spirit is channeled through the work you do. To unseat negative thinking that interferes with your success, refer to these affirmations about the work environment and shift to a positive and productive mode.

Overwork

I am overworked because I choose to be out of balance. Today I begin a course of action that aligns my work schedule with healthy living. From this day forward, I am committed to balancing my work and personal life. I am created from an image of balance.

Bringing Personal Strife to Work

Today I set sail on a more disciplined course of action to inspire others in this organization. My greatest contribution is showing others how well I can weather the storm. I resolve to bring a higher level of awareness to those around me as I set a positive example of how to manage life's difficulties. My heart and mind are strong. All is well in the world.

Feeling Like a Number in a Large Organization

Every person on this planet, every soul is a unique spark of the Divine. My contribution is important because no one has my unique essence. I contribute to the greater good through this organization because I am a vital element of the universe. My presence is a gift to others.

DISCRIMINATION

I have experienced discrimination because others are unwilling to let their soul recognize my soul. We are all composed of the same perfect substance. I forgive others for their lack of insight and know that this experience is meant to show me a part of the human condition. I am a beloved and unique individual who is empowered by divine love and light.

For more affirmations, see my companion book, *The Women's Book of Empowerment: 323 Affirmations That Change Everyday Problems into Moments of Potential* (The Goddess Network Press, 2005). Available through any major online book retailer or at www.thegoddessnetwork.net.

Taking Spiritual Inventory:
Allow Spirit to Navigate Your Workday

Analyze

Does workplace imbalance come from external circumstances or feelings we bring into our workplaces? Is it the responsibility of our employers to set an agenda for us to realize our potential? Is it all up to us? Do you feel a lack of connection between what you do for a living and your soul work? How do we bring those two ideas into balance? In your work, do you feel you demonstrate your true self? Ask yourself:

* Am I exposed to negativity in my job? When my colleagues or customers do not realize their potential, do I attempt to fill the gap on my own? Is it possible to allow spirit to help fill *my* day? Am I the source of my own negativity?
* Do I compromise my value set during the course of my workday? If so, how?
* How do we cultivate our "light" and let it pervade the workplace? How do we cultivate the light in others, while working with people who have hugely diverse philosophies and religions? Is it necessary for us to all believe in the same ideas? Why or why not?
* Does your workplace, organization, or family have a value set that does not reflect what women want and need? Do you think women's values differ from men's? If so, how?
* Have our organizations evolved to accommodate a value set that works for men and not for women? If so, how? Do you see it changing? What cultural, political, or world events will influence the way we "organize"?
* Look into the future and predict what organizations will be like

in a hundred years. Do you believe you can change the future with what you offer? Do you feel your work energy reaches around the world? Why or why not?

✻ If you are an organizational leader, is it possible to institute a new positive image of what the organization's collective energy – the energy of the employees – is attempting to do? Can you help channel people's most positive aspects of themselves? If so, how? If not, what prevents you?

Affirm

You are part of a powerful time in world history by being at the hub of positive change. You have an opportunity to inspire others to rise above their circumstances and reach higher ground. Taking your spiritual truth to work every day is an internal as well as external experience, because we must *demonstrate* our God-self, or our true self, to feel good about what we do.

Affirm that you are strong and capable. Write an affirmation about your female strengths and what values you'd like to guide your work life.

Walk the Talk

List the realistic actions you will take to allow your highest and most beloved ideals to transfer into your workplace. If you are in a leadership position and could change your organization in any way to allow a balance of power, what would you do? What would you visualize every day? If a thought can be manifested, why is it still so difficult for anyone to institute change?

Share the Spirit

Create dialogue to foster spiritual energy wherever you work. With each action you take, ask yourself: Is my integrity and spirit alive during my workday? Am I nurturing a positive and loving image of the Divine by also being positive and loving? Do I have the big picture frequently in my mind? How can I show others the importance of a reverence for nature, nurturing, compassion, and intuitive action? Make a list of what you can do to bring your vision of balance between the concepts of male and female within your workplace.

Male or Female
Idea/Value

How It Would Bring
Balance to My Organization

_____   _____
_____   _____
_____   _____
_____   _____
_____   _____
_____   _____
_____   _____
_____   _____
_____   _____
_____   _____
_____   _____
_____   _____
_____   _____
_____   _____
_____   _____
_____   _____
_____   _____
_____   _____
_____   _____

As I search for divine love,
I find it inside myself.
My understanding and
acceptance of love makes
my light shine brighter.
I am supported by a
higher power in every
aspect of my life.

The Divine Feminine

Bring Mother God
into Your Work
and Life

Reviving the Goddess in You

God is simple. He's so good, She's so good. Until I saw both in me,
I did not fully understand myself...and feel complete.

– Caryn, spiritual retreat attendee

Women never cease to amaze me when they rally at impromptu
gatherings to reignite the bonds of their ancient female past.
Recently, I was invited to join a group of women on a trip to the
American southwest. I knew only the trip planner. Some arrived
as friendship partners or business partners; others were taking a
brief hiatus from being mother, wife, fundraiser, curator, marketing analyst, or teacher. Others came for meditative time and long
walks, seizing the day to reconnect with their bodies through better eating or exercise. Our only commitment: eat together at least
once during the week.

Surprisingly, in six days this group went from strangers to sis-
terhood, laughing like old friends, sharing conversation about
marriages, children, and spiritual development. Unknowingly,
we granted ourselves permission to deeply explore one another's minds with the intention of learning, and nothing more.
Unthreatened by our diversity, we developed a dialogue, and we
were both shocked and entertained by everyone's perspective. By
the time we participated in a drumming circle on the final evening, we beat our instruments as if it were the last day on earth,
rhythm makers connecting land and sky, our dancing selves somewhere in between.

By the time the last flame was extinguished, a sense of community existed which was nothing less than magical: a pledge of

support and understanding as we re-entered our individual lives. Our sacred circle was inadvertently cast. And a grounded, unstructured, woman-affirming spirituality arose from empti-ness, as a consequence of creating space for wisdom to emerge.

What is it about a woman-gathering that *empowers* women? It's molding col-lective ideas into something that makes sense; the telling of stories; inhaling a woman's worldly view-point and not a man's. It's about enhancing our judgment on what to let go and what to pack in the suitcase for the journey home. A woman-gathering is an opportunity to place sticky notes on those areas of our lives where we've lacked true self-awareness, alerting us to why we have been taking too much direction from external circumstances and not enough from a sense of our own creative power. Our individual and collective strength is greatly dimin-ished when our minds race with what needs to be done and whose needs need to be met next, with little or no time to revisit the *mean-ing* of what we're doing. As a result, we wander, letting life move us instead of choosing where we want to move life.

> I watch people all day long, listen to their problems. Women are a mile deep, compared with the men. When you get them away from competing for the men, there is a lot of group spirit. They seem totally different.
>
> *Fay, bartender*

Reviving our past extends far beyond analyzing the happen-stance of the immediate. It goes back to a time when tribal sis-terhood existed, when women helped one another find wisdom within everyday experiences, when making spiritual room for self-discovery and renewal was as necessary as breathing. I believe we are born with a need to gather ancient women's wisdom from all walks of life and apply it to our private expeditions. Women long to share stories of tragedy and success, to weep, giggle, and feel better about adversity, while comparing notes about how to improve our own thinking and change our individual worlds through relationships and work.

We must search openly for illumination in an effort to reinvent the present. It's what returns us to present-moment awareness. This idea exemplifies the meaning of the Goddess: the deep
connection we have to the present because our environment, in the
form of relationships or struggles, is a mirror reflection of what we
think. She is about finding meaning in the sacredness and fecun-
dity of the human experience.

The Goddess helps us arrive at present-moment awareness
because the entire idea of existing within Her is about the here
and now, not the afterlife. The Goddess is about *spirit awareness* of
being in a body while accepting temporal limitations with a limitless mind. Fluctuating between those two ideas demonstrates our
potential as human beings. When we allow the Goddess to run wild
inside us, our lives become an exercise in self-awareness, because
we find acceptance and pleasure in witnessing the rebirth of ourselves. Hence power and wisdom grow, as does our confidence.

When women believe they are divine, a beloved image of power
from both God and Goddess, they will realize their empowered
state, through sharing mythology, stories, and the meaning of
woman-rituals that bring them back to center.

Grow a Balanced, Empowered Self

Generating woman-power to overcome inevitable everyday problems, or perhaps deeper issues of self-love, acceptance, or forgiveness, is about knowing the spirit-power within at an intimate level.
The word *empowerment* means power put into action. When you
reach the point of empowerment, you operate from an unfathom-
able sense of spiritual balance, a profound knowingness that you
are composed of the All and are able to use it in the real world. It's
impossible to generate self-love or put any spiritual principle to
work until you fully embrace all aspects of who you are. Loving self

is about loving spirit. Your power to effect change and cope is your inherent spirit-power put into action.

To be balanced and joyful people who love freely, we must feel our sense of power at the very core of our being. But true empowerment is not based upon feelings of superiority from *being* either a man or a woman, or from membership in an exclusive organization. Empowerment stems from belonging to the "divine I." You are a rendition of divine power from the minute you are born, with an invitation to draw at will from that account, which is always in balance. But to launch thoughts into reality, we need to rely upon images of a higher power that exemplify our true selves. If we want to feel balanced, with an all-encompassing sense of self-love, we need to believe that we arrive as an example of a balanced image of the Divine. It is our natural state.

> Truthfully, in my religion I've never really thought about anything else other than Jesus. It's just what I know.
>
> *Kim, Presbyterian Church deacon*

To some extent, we've been doing this for centuries, because religion nudges us toward a higher power who is compassionate and loving, creating goodness, managing the universe with love. We identify with divine imagery by "being" like father and son, because it helps close the conceptual gap between who we are as humans and our spiritual source, that which constitutes us. It's important to see ourselves reflected in the Divine because we have relationships with those ideas – they often validate and guide our earth journeys. Our knowledge of *being* divine must emanate from us at a very deep level, becoming our mental equivalent. We are the All, as we've already discussed, so we are also God. We are our spirit-power.

But our spirit-power is a *balanced* image of creation, with both masculine and feminine ideas, because we are one and the same; in fact, we are left and right halves of the brain, reconciling the intellectual and the intuitive, comprising both ordered and chaotic activities. As humans, we're simultaneously active and receptive, inheriting a physiological harmony at the chromosomal level. We are all composed of both masculine and feminine. If we continue to conceptualize the All with gender duality as we've been doing for ages, it's about time we recognized ourselves in a balanced image of divinity, one that includes both He and She.

> When I sit down to write, I just let it flow. On the days I have a clear head, and quit dragging all kinds of past junk into my mind, those are the days I do my best work. Maybe that means I am channeling a higher power.
>
> *Cae, writer*

Currently people are spending a lot of time talking about balance. We're astounded that everyone around us leads such lopsided lives of frenzy. Everyone is looking for a remedy to rebalance life, especially women. If the world is a manifestation of what we think, what we see is an unbalanced reflection of our own spiritual composition. The spiritual equation we are using to fuel our thought process to manifest reality is out of balance. We can't bring that power into our reality because we don't recognize it in ourselves.

Self-image stems from how we visualize the Divine. Without identification with *both* aspects of divinity, our world will never even closely resemble anything in balance. Until we recognize that the Divine is at work *through* us, a divine mother as well as a divine father present and at work in our lives, humanity will not feel empowered. Certainly, women will not reach their full potential. Even men need to revitalize their feminine side to live more balanced lives. Our institutions need it. And it's overdue.

Construct a Female Bridge to a Divine Self-Image

Women have special needs when it comes to empowered living. To produce desired outcomes in life, even miracles, we need to unpeel the layers of old, negative thought patterns to create change, but we must also merge this belief system with the conscious awareness of our own divinity. Constructing the female bridge between spirit-power and new realities, leading to happy and balanced lives, is about seeing yourself in God, *believing* you are divine, claiming full ownership of the All inside. You don't need permission from a church, parents, or spouses.

Women don't feel divine because their relationship to God is restricted by old mental programs, some developed in their current lifetimes but others passed on through generations as what science now labels genetic patterns of thinking. In theory, we are predisposed to certain thoughts, courtesy of our heritage, that are reinforced by absorbing our parents' and grandparents' attitudes. Before we leave the nest, we are faced with the task of overriding those patterns if we want to forge ahead and create the world *we* want. Although the jury is still out on genetic thought inheritance, like any other ingrained program that is self-determined or claimed through our environment, the attitudes of our elders do affect our perception of what a person can do.

For generations, women have not seen themselves reflected in the image of a God whose policies were derived from men's values, not women's. Religious dogma, extracted in the form of society's rules about the available list of women's choices, fits with a vision that made sense to men, not women. In the God category, women have lacked a power broker for far too long. Although many people can transcend gender-based images of the Divine and go direct to the All, current culture still has a lot of old, negative programming, dictated by a male deity, that sees women as a less-valued species. We need to revive from history and from a feminist gospel a symbol of empowerment that makes sense.

The Goddess has been there all along, in our scriptures and world history, buried as a consequence of struggles for political power and the rise of newer religions. It's time to rediscover Her, as a stepping stone to the big fundamental reason for being here, which is to realize our own creative potential. We are here to demonstrate our thoughts, and that includes what we think of ourselves as individuals and a group of souls.

MAKE ROOM FOR YOUR DIVINE SELF BY CONFRONTING FEAR AND SELF-DOUBT

Without changing our emotional response to an environmental condition, we close the door on new experiences because there is comfort in doing things the same. When we step outside old boundaries, we are in uncharted territory, and often fear is our buddy. Fear comes from hiding truth – the truth of past experiences we have undergone individually and together, as a culture or a society. There is no room for empowerment where fear exists. Releasing fear in favor of empowerment requires conscious awareness of our thoughts, which requires changing our perception of the world so we can realize the effect we want; and knowing the common factor in empowerment is not age, gender, or color. It is that all human beings are divine. If we are holding ourselves back from empowerment, it is because of these two things: we don't want to believe we can change the world, nor do we believe we are truly divine.

> I really like to see doctors get patients to take charge of their disease and help them think they can beat it, not be helpless and dependent.
> I love my job when I see people who have great attitude. It makes my job worthwhile.
>
> *Marie, nurse*

Despite fear's constraints, it is still possible to individually choose change, no matter what society says. It's achievable through affirmative thinking and conscious awareness. You must choose to reject old messages from the past in favor of positive and empowered ideas; but do so deliberately, fueled with knowledge of the past that helps the mind reconcile these mental programs.

Choosing change starts with uncovering deep-seated assumptions about a woman's place in the world. I've interviewed hundreds of women on this subject, and despite the level of opportunity women have in this society, they still cling to the notion that they are not divine, not of the same "God substance" as men. They still don't feel as capable as men.

Once women uncover why they don't feel empowered, they can move past this old notion, allowing their minds to create space for new thoughts and experiences based upon the present. That is why we must first study our own history. It gives the intellect a basis for analysis. It's not about dredging up old stories of discrimination; it's about making comparisons that make sense to the mind about why women need to move forward with better ways to think and live.

Although it is beneficial to recognize the less inspiring historical events on record, women still can't confront all our fears this way. It's good to dig through world archives and unearth things we never want to experience again. But our culture has a habit of getting stuck in the analysis. We regurgitate war stories, tales of lynch mobs, and other accounts of awful human behavior, then remember (re-experience) the same reactions to those events, over and over. We think we can rectify past atrocities by getting emotionally stuck there and existing within that state as a tribute to those who suffered. Getting stuck in old ideas is like a protest rally that never ends. If we cling too tightly to the past, we will produce the same outcomes in our current experiences.

Why don't women want to admit they are divine? When they cross that conceptual bridge, there would no longer be anyone else to blame for their circumstances, no longer a reason why they cannot change. Ouch! If women want change, they have to do the work. Life is created by our own intentions. We move closer to a collective vision of our God-self when we believe in our self-worth.

So what are we so fearful of exploring?

The Goddess has been extremely misunderstood. Most people have a limited knowledge base to rely upon when the subject arises. We are held captive by old ideas of witches, sacrifice, or magic rituals associated with the devil, fears held in our group consciousness as well as programs that each of us may be carrying on our own. Until we overcome our fear of the Goddess, which produces strong emotional reactions in people who feel threatened by the idea, we will never be able to integrate a balanced image of divinity as a model for our own behavior, as souls experiencing the mystery of life.

> I don't know anything about the Goddess. Isn't the Goddess all those Greek statues, like Zeus? Or maybe a woman who is feeling beautiful, like inner beauty?
>
> *Rita, mother, wife, school volunteer*

Feeling empowered grows from letting go of fears of believing we are divine. Men have an easier time believing they are divine substance, because religions have been created by men. They celebrate male-oriented ideas and use a male referent system, and a man can identify with their creative power because God is He. Women must make more of a conceptual leap because we don't hear about God the Mother. An image of the Goddess, or God the Mother, is the intermediate step, a power symbol for a woman's acceptance of her own divinity. Once they embrace female deity within themselves, women will feel empowered.

FEAR OF THE FEMININE PRINCIPLE

Revitalizing the Goddess through prayer, affirmation, and even religious practice does challenge people's perspectives. I am no longer surprised at the resistance to this idea by women who are filled with fear, unwilling to explore outside their safe boundaries.

The subject of the Goddess, so aptly documented by archaeology and religious scholars, is considered nothing less than compelling. Goddess history, myth, and thealogy (the feminist version of theology) provide a foundation for Judeo-Christian values. Many feel the idea competes for room on their already established but divided path to the light – a path that definitely has right and wrong sides to drive on.

At a luncheon years ago, I sat next to a woman who expressed interest in my work as a writer and lecturer. "What do you do for a living?" she asked, sharing with me that she was a Catholic woman of faith. When I told her I was teaching women positive thinking and self-empowerment through the concept of Mother God, she became interested and her eyes widened. I talked about the period of history when the Goddess, whose worship most likely included women's participation in sacred sexual practices in community temples, was a target of the Hebrew power structure. It is evident to scholars that getting rid of the matrilineal descent system, as well as all the sexy stuff, gave men greater access to land and control of government. The customs and symbolism of the ancient goddess religions didn't fit with the changing times.

In fact, the various books of the Bible were influenced by the shift to patriarchy and by the political aims of priests and other policy makers, especially those of the invading patrilineal Hebrews. Because Levite theology did not have room for women who were sexually autonomous and who held a very high community status, women's rites – as well as their rights – were eradicated. As I continued my history lesson, I asked, Isn't it possible that the absence of the Goddess today is a reason why our culture is seriously imbalanced?

As we got into a discussion of Mary, the virgin mother of Christ, an assimilated goddess in the Catholic religion, this woman's eyes narrowed down to slits. She lowered her head at me, pointing her imaginary, battle-ready antlers, and actually growled.

> I got tired of going to church, singing songs about men and hearing about being a sinner. I used to think there was something wrong with me. So now I'm a church CEO – Christmas and Easter only.
>
> *Marva, event planner*

"Be careful, Charlene," she warned. "Be very, *very* careful." Perhaps I shocked her by mentioning sex. Despite violent rape scenes in movies and the widespread use of sexual themes to market products, we can still be astoundingly inhibited. Or perhaps she could not imagine allowing Mother God to share the dais with Father and Son. I suppose mixing sex and religion, with a little controversy on property ownership thrown in, was not such a good topic for lunch conversation.

Sexuality and the authority of the church are intertwined subjects worthy of exploration because they challenge our perceptions as women. Women should question the existing state of affairs and feel good about doing so. They still lack confidence and carry deep-seated inadequacies fueled by fear: fear of their own sexuality, fear that they are naturally dirty and sinful, or born in sin. Many women feel they are less than worthy because someone established long ago that they were not to worship, marry, or have children unless sanctioned by law or the church.

Women have been taught to be fearful of their intuitive natures and were told that their religious rites, which included the worship of female deity, conflicted with community order. Over the centuries, the undervaluing of women created dependency not only upon men but also upon institutions. As a society, we've spent an inordinate amount of time insisting on women's compliance. Our old programming makes us fearful of causing disruption, which conflicts with our inherent value system. Although we've come a long way, the residual effects are still evident: many women feel invalid without a man. We need a lot of approval and spend too much time and effort getting it, judging by the average woman's expenditures on cosmetics, computerized dating services, hair removal, diet remedies, fashion, and therapy. Not a very empowering place to be.

The subject of female deity brings to the surface ideas we have not been willing to recognize in ourselves. Our discomfort with the topic says a lot about a lack of self-worth we share as individuals. Through running The Goddess Network, I have gained a well-rounded perspective on observing fear of the feminine. I am continually astounded by the fear factor. It could be the subject of an entirely new version of a prime-time television show.

Our business provides women with live and online programs for exploring new avenues of empowerment to revitalize their power within. I've noticed the difficulty people have with the Goddess, a concept that may require them to step outside the boundaries of religion or other mythologies, because it challenges their feelings of safety. Instead of exploring spirituality with love and an imagination, they want confirmation that they belong to an idea greater than themselves, and that a competing viewpoint is a threat rather than an opportunity to learn. People in our society are fearful of their bodies, sex, Satan, demonic energies, snakes, temptation, going to hell, the dark side of the moon, and not belonging to the "right" religion. And fear is found across the board, in both men and women.

I've had former job applicants demand that I burn all the paperwork for their applications, citing the "new age religion" on our website as blasphemy. Competent researchers in my academic field of simulation architecture, who have respected my work as a social scientist for years, now refuse to work with me because they say they have a personal relationship with Christ, and any association with what I talk about is an invitation to the devil. Female writers decline to write about me because they say the assignment conflicts with their religion, and male computer programmers, when they read our material, refuse to work on my website because they say their relationship with Jesus doesn't permit them to discuss such ideas. Fear, in its wide variety, is amplified when it comes to the subject of female deity. Why are we so touchy about the subject?

FEAR OF EMPOWERING OUR WOMEN-YOUTH

> No, we can't look into some parts of history. Some things are just better left alone so we can forget. Besides, you can't go against the church. This country is 80 percent Christian, you know.
>
> *Karen, shopkeeper*

Perhaps we don't examine history enough to look for answers. Humanity's lessons are learned from reflection on the past, which can heal old wounds in our group soul. Examining history also lends insight on customs and attitudes. The process helps us weed out leftover thought patterns that don't serve the higher good, lending logic to school-sanctioned museum trips where our kids spend time with Hitler's ugly enslavements and atrocities.

However, I see a big problem with how we direct the intellectual focus of our youth during their impressionable, opinion-forming years. It's highly subjective and bows to the pressure of an authoritarian, Christian past. If we want to remember what we didn't do so well together, as an exercise in learning to get it right from now on, we ought to bring forward a more complete viewpoint from women, showing what it might have been like to have their religious images and rites exterminated.

We gloss over the real reason for the burning of the libraries in Alexandria in 391 C.E., and for other events surrounding the destruction of the intelligentsia and the suppression of Pagan religion. Paganism was a spirituality that was not some primitive, rural superstition but a more mystical expression that inspired thinkers, artists, philosophers, and innovators of the ancient world, many of whom were women. At the heart of Pagan philosophy is an understanding that all things are one: a mystical union with spirit that included belief in a divine feminine. But the systematic elimination of virtually all forms of feminine imagery of God, labeled heresies by orthodox tradition, and the institution of literalist Christianity over time caused a deep and painful division between men and women. As scholars are discovering, the church authoritatively proclaimed that the feminine was inferior and so dangerous that it must be strictly controlled.

Even in more modern times, our male predecessors, the policy makers and organizational leaders, were deeply immersed in male-oriented religions. In the eighteenth and nineteenth centuries, discrimination prevented women from self-expression, and family values left over from church doctrines prohibited female leadership, economic autonomy, and birth control. Judaism, Christianity, and Islam all include dogma legitimizing the subordination of women. Burying the divine feminine, or eliminating any mention of it in scriptures sanctioned by the church, is all part of our checkered past. According to many male scholars, the Goddess was nothing more than a fertility symbol. Somehow, we've lost a rich theological perspective that encompasses women's mystical roots. Why don't we want to discuss it?

> When I went to school, nobody talked about feminism or any woman topics. If you wanted to talk about those ideas, you had to form an after-school club. Of course, you had to get permission from the school first. It just seemed like too much effort, and there wasn't any leadership anyway.
>
> *Betty, Class of 1962,*
> *lifelong student*

Hearing the robust herstory of female religion and philosophy, or even of women leaders who have broken traditional molds from the past, is empowering to our women-youth because it teaches them to question. It challenges their perspective about their own religious orientation and helps them decide whether they resonate with what they are hearing. Empowerment is about self-reflection, learning about the effects of negative thought patterns, and then mobilizing to correct them, whether internally or societally. It's not about complaining about how long it took to get the vote or to receive equal protection under the law. Empowerment requires discussion of what has produced negative outcomes for women, especially the discrimination that continues today. At its root were negative thought patterns stemming from fear.

It is evident that middle and high school educators refuse to take a broader view on women's empowerment, sticking to topics sprinkled around the edges of a traditional curriculum such as "the first woman to ..." (name the achievement) when they ought to be expanding the world religions program instead. Ancient goddess religion, Paganism, Wicca, mysticism, Gnosticism, or anything remotely considered new thought (or, in this case, really old thought) isn't incorporated into world religions class. Apparently the experts can't agree on where the unseating of the feminine principle in favor of an all-male God fits into the religion curriculum, so it's tossed over the fence to history class. However, history from a woman's perspective is usually absent from that curriculum too. It's unfortunate that this type of discourse remains unheard until college. Why are we so afraid to allow our youth to explore these topics?

Certainly it can be difficult to present the subject to wide-eyed youngsters who may hear at home that witches are to be feared. Stimulating a discussion on why women and other non-Christian believers were burned at the stake or sent to torturous deaths opens the door wide to commentary not only on ethical human behavior but mainly on why societies keep using religion to obtain control. Even today, many people believe that goddess worship is about consorting with the devil and casting magic spells. Satan, the ultimate form of fear that somehow this culture cannot fully unseat, appears to hold people captive still.

Discussion of women's religion and the eradication of the goddess religions would empower our women-youth, providing a sense of joy that we all lived through some difficult times. But, more important, it would open discussion on why our culture insists on destroying some of our very best ideas. Our youth can no longer survive intellectually with compartmentalization of knowledge. It's the big, interdisciplinary mix of ideas that keeps the human brain evolving.

Further, the spiritual revival of the old values of goddess-loving communities, which are actually values based upon the structure of old temple communities, has been a pretty good management and governing plan. It's not surprising that in the past decade, organizational consultants have been stressing shared and decentralized leadership, intuitive decision making, egalitarianism, compassion, and nurturing of the human spirit, values that create more productive and profitable management teams and communities. These female values, or goddess values, provide an extremely efficient community structure. It's time we grew up, focused on the rich body of knowledge we call the past, examined it from all angles, and quit wasting our energy on fear.

Sex, Property, and Power

In order to reconcile the past and the present and move forward, we ought to let ourselves be captivated by what was hidden for so long, in scripture and history books. There was a vast and theologically complex female religion flourishing thousands of years before the advent of Judaism, Christianity, and the classical age of Greece. Writers of the Judeo-Christian Bible skimmed over the subject of the female deity who was held sacred by the neighbors of the Hebrews in Canaan, Babylon, and Egypt. In Egypt, the Hebrews knew of the worship of the Goddess, called Isis or Hathor. Of all goddess-loving cultures on record, the Canaanites deserve special mention for their experience of the eradication of the feminine principle.

When the Hebrews entered Canaan, they found a country rich with the tradition of Mother God worship. The goddess Ashtoreth (meaning "tree of life") or Astarte (meaning "that which issues from the womb") was known as the Great Godddess in Canaan and embraced as a deity. During biblical times, as had been customary for thousands of years in Sumer and Babylon, many women lived within temple complexes. Temples were entire economic systems unto themselves, keeping land and herds. They functioned as city offices.

Women who resided within the temples and practiced sexual customs of the faith took lovers from the community to pay honor to the Goddess. Temple sex was considered a holy act, a tribute to the life-generating principle. The divine feminine principle was similarly worshipped elsewhere in the Near and Middle East through prayer, ritual, and sexual practices. According to scholars, many of these *qadishtu*, sanctified women or holy women in the Canaanite language, appeared to be from wealthy families and well accepted in the community. Children born to these sacred women of the Goddess inherited the property and titles of their mothers, as they were of questionable paternity. The matrilineal line of descent was part of the social structure of the community.

> I teach numbers all day, but that won't be what life is all about for these kids. I'd like to see them spend a little more time with nature, cultural issues, learn how to think for themselves. That is what will make them successful.
>
> *Jody, math teacher*

Such traditions were condemned by Levite-led Hebrews, who denounced them as wicked and depraved. Levite priests devised their own concept of sexual morality: premarital virginity for women and marital fidelity for women (not men), in order to have total control over the knowledge of paternity. Enforcement of patriarchal attitudes concerning sexual ownership of women put an end to festivals and all rejoicing with reference to the Queen of Heaven. It involved merciless slaughters of those refusing to accept Yahweh (or Jehovah) as their new God. Punishments, in the form of stoning, burning, or other tortures, were severe. According to the Bible, these laws were instituted at the time of Moses, shortly before the Hebrew tribes invaded Canaan, starting a long and ugly battle that continued through the Roman and early Christian eras.

As a consequence of the condemnation of goddess-worshipping cultures in what we now call the Old Testament, Judaic monotheism lacked any images of the feminine principle. Because Hebrew priests eradicated the Canaanite rituals (which included women as priestesses) and enforced strict codes of sexual behavior, they could not justify allowing females to share the dais. Even to maintain peace, it was unacceptable to link the Goddess, or female deity, to Yahweh as an equal.

Priestesses, whose power was perceived as a direct connection to the Divine, were conduits of holy spirit. This position validated them as having characteristics of being divine, and they commanded a great deal of power in the community. Women who were in the habit of providing advice at shrines were seen as fit counselors and priests since they were intuitive and emotional, both viewed as good qualities. Formerly considered mediums for divine revelation, women were chased out of the temples, and their practices were later referred to by male scholars as "obscure astrological cults."

Goddess religion was *not* about wild women running rampant in their communities having random sex with the men, as many male theologians would have us believe. Mother God worship was a rich tradition, addressing the natural rhythms of the earth and the symbolic implications of life's transformative changes. Unfortunately, the fundamental idea of the divine feminine principle linking a transcendent deity with the sacred aspect of human experience was slowly disassembled.

Although the Queen of Heaven, who represented the earthly evolutionary path of the soul, was no longer a major presence in divine imagery, elements did survive. While Yahweh appointed the people of Israel as spiritual partners in overcoming political adversaries and competing spiritual traditions such as the Canaanite goddess culture, Sophia, the Queen of Heaven, became the bride of Yahweh, or his heavenly consort. She is hidden in the Bible in the term "holy wisdom," a connection later rejected by Jewish literalists.

THE SHIFT TO PATRIARCHAL VALUES

Over time, the emphasis shifted from images of God as represented in nature (feminine) to a transcendent image (masculine) in order to inspire consciousness. The objective was to encourage people to focus on a dimension *beyond* appearance. Our bodies, once revered and celebrated in temples serving as the center of communities, became shameful and dirty, tempting men's satanic impulses. Women, the human instrument of the Goddess, were contained in order to empower men through creation myths. The concept of the sacred marriage of intellect and emotion - exemplified in the ritual of sexual union, quite normal and socially acceptable at the time - was suddenly feared and tightly controlled.

The development of Christianity, centuries later, was a colorful journey, encompassing political struggles and the absorption of cultural streams of many traditions. Christianity adopted many elements from Judaism but was also heavily influenced by the Gnostics, whose mystic philosophers desired experiential knowledge of truth. Ancient mystical teachings were actually a synthesis of Jewish and Pagan mythologies. Through symbolism, allegory, and some really good stories, the mystics had their own interpretations on the subject of the divine feminine. These themes, mainly reiterating the permanence of our essential nature, were about the journey to God or the path we travel to the discovery of the authentic self. The path included the knowledge that we are *not* separate individuals, and that to evolve, we must embrace our earth existence given by the Goddess.

Early Christians were interested in the transformation of consciousness, a spiritual philosophy leading to an initiation into *gnosis* – direct experiential knowledge of God. It was a deeper, more mystical interpretation of the inner knowledge that we are all one. To reach enlightenment through gnosis, we need to understand that no self-knowledge is possible without temporary identification with the body, in a journey of awakening courtesy of the Mother Goddess. To achieve a state of self-knowledge, we must embrace the idea of the mystical marriage of our essential natures: consciousness (spirit, Father, God) with psyche (soul or the temporal bodily experience, Mother, Goddess). The divine masculine and feminine would at last achieve unity and completion.

> When I am in our group, I feel a connection with all women and the power of the universe. I need it. When I go back to the real world, I feel great. I can do my job so much better.
>
> *Elizabeth, priestess, lodge member, and sales manager for an audiovisual company*

As suppression of the feminine principle continued through the fourth century, Roman churches gathered the spiritual outliers into a literalist, official religion, eradicating the concept of the Mother, who by then was seen as Sophia the wise goddess. The church set out to unify Christianity by force, with laws that were intolerant of alternative intellectual theories of our spiritual origins or of anyone practicing "partnership spirituality." Originally, the division of the sexes was thought of as a primal duality (the source of creation). This duality, when made one as in the act of love, would bring the bliss of symbolic union. But instead of men and women embracing each other in the spirit of eternal fellowship, as expressions of God and Goddess, mainstream religion wound up with a spiritual battleground where the sexes are stratified, both intellectually and spiritually.

This division continued to threaten later versions of goddess-Pagan religion, which emphasized community values and a grounded spirituality. They believed (and still do) in shared priestly power and models of rotating leadership, intuitive healing, and divination as intermediaries to spirit. Women, psychics, and life givers, formerly viewed as channels of Mother God, were disenfranchised through persecution and extermination, including many who were educators, priestesses, and healers in their own Pagan communities. Although these brutal transfers of power from women to men are well documented, society still seems to accept unthinkingly the devaluation of the sacred feminine.

Today's philosophers are reminding us of these implications: that our withdrawal from nature, to favor a solely transcendent God, is the reason we have lost many of our ethical values, which stem from our participation in earthly life. Although it's too late to return to the goddess religions of old and rebuild the temples, we should reconsider the foundation of religious structures. It translates into our value base. Because we do not include a metaphor of Mother God (earth) in our referent system, what goes unexamined is our attitude toward the environment, and the attention we need to pay to our soul-vehicle, which is the body, in the form of healthy diets that promote longevity.

We need lively discussion and spiritual discourse on the concept of property ownership and why we still can't share ideas. We remain fueled by fear and believe power stems from ownership of something or someone. We also retain our belief in the concept of lack. Until we get it right, males and females will never take care of one another well, let alone a planet of nations. Women, and female images of the Divine, don't have to be in charge, and neither do men's ideas. By now, we ought to be able to shake hands and meet halfway. It's important for the survival of our species.

Our herstory, as a contribution to an evolving world culture, is so very rich in simple wisdom on the subject of empowerment. It has huge spiritual value for everyone, worthy of a celebration that breaks through the lines we've drawn as a consequence of our religious evolution. We should know by now that possessions, in the form of land and children or even someone's virginal state, do not make us powerful. Nor does anything of a material nature, nor control of another individual. What gives us the ability to survive in any circumstance and come out ahead is the knowledge that we are *as divine* as the person standing next to us, no matter the gender, color, religion. The concept of divine woman as an instrument of the All is re-emerging to speak the message loud and clear, in an effort to rebalance our world. We are already celebrating it in our retreats and workshops, grooming ourselves for widespread institutional change. The Goddess within is bursting forth, and by stepping into this vision, we do not *become* empowered. We exist within our conscious awareness, living life by *being* empowered.

We need to revisit these positive thoughts in holidays, holy days, and religious institutions. We need to affirm them in greeting cards, in our mantras, in posters hanging in our corporate lunchrooms. Men and women have been given the same soul substance since the beginning and were meant to be channels of divine power, not just in churches but in every aspect of life, from the living room to the boardroom and the bedroom. We are equally divine because we were made in images of both a Father and a Mother God, and we must learn to demonstrate shared power on earth. That is, quite simply, our greatest challenge in this world of opposites, apparent in every corner of our lives. In the interest of collaboration, we must all move forward and leave our comfort zones in favor of harnessing the power of our authentic self.

> It's so hard to teach people how to love themselves. Everyone is self-critical, always finding some reason why they can't accept who they are.
>
> *Sheryl, personal coach*

What Is Self-Worth?

Self-worth has its entire foundation in self-love, which is really how you feel about being an individual spark of the Divine. If you cannot generate a love of your God-self, you'll never be able to feel worthy, and no amount of blaming past circumstances, people, or policy will fix it. Patching up our psyches – in the form of liposuction, exercise, blaming our parents or the weather – is only a way we choose to avoid self-love. Substitutes for self-love, such as poor relationships, overwork, overweight, and a host of other daytime talk-show ailments, are more ways we avoid loving ourselves. We get hung up on the external circumstances. But our soul journey *always* includes obstacles to rediscovering our own self-worth in order to make us appreciate our God-self with greater passion.

Without self-love, you have not placed any value upon your worth as an individual spark of divine power. You haven't recognized that your power is already within you. Your true self is your spirit-power, unlimited and uncontained. When you know this, you'll be filled with your own sense of potential and will rise every day with a feeling of self-worth and purpose.

Every woman or girl needs to be told she is absolutely gorgeous, from the inside out. We need to welcome our periods, celebrate our hips and breasts, dance our emotions without any guilt or embarrassment, and be encouraged to rely upon our own decision-making power. All messages we receive in our families as children, whether or not they are integrated in a spiritual support system, contribute to our feelings of self-worth as adults. They often come from automatic programs we have running in our heads, with far-reaching effects. It's complicated because our society highly values physical beauty. As children, we rely upon those around us for instruction on how to build self-confidence in our physical image first, because it's tangible.

When families don't celebrate the female gender through rites of passage, girls in their formative years cannot step into valuable, self-defining, community-serving leadership roles. They need to know that their place in the world is validated by a higher power. And when powerful female imagery is not valued in society, women can't achieve their potential. Without these two basic elements in society's support system, females will settle for things they don't want. They develop a dependency on outside approval that permeates relationships from marriage to the workplace.

Why don't women feel worthy? Sometimes the pains of inadequacy are lesions left over from old family values. I talk to many women who feel they still give away their power to outdated ideas or people; they are still imprisoned by the need for approval from male authority figures, even when common sense tells them to rely upon their own intuition and wisdom. If women's home cultures included men who had the ultimate say-so, they still carry well-concealed pangs of self-doubt about their capabilities and what they deserve.

Although we hate to admit it, the stain of many creation myths gave us a head start on self-doubt and apologizing for who we are. Nothing is more absurd than holy doctrines that have sold the masses on the concept of woman being far less divine than man by way of her "responsibility" for the sufferings of humanity. Because of this, many women still believe they should rightfully be dominated by wiser men. But all humans were created in the image of *both* their creators, the ultimate power source.

Statements carefully designed to devalue women and cited by our elders or taught in churches, schools, synagogues, or homes *did* influence our self-worth as women, if they were translated into family values and behaviors that required us to acquiesce to survive. If Dad was not to be questioned, and Mom went along with the program, we learned silence at an early age. We denied our creativity or had short-sighted visions of what we could accomplish.

It was unspoken acceptance of our own inadequacy as women. If our mothers were incapable of defining themselves as independent thinkers and doers who could champion positive contributions that females made to the world, girls were left to navigate through years of subliminal messages of non-deserving, carried well into adulthood.

RECOVER BY RELEASING OLD MESSAGES FROM THE PAST

Everyone has a direct connection to the Divine, not through some intermediary but on a path accessible from within. It's absolutely necessary to teach kids how to access their "Divine I" at an early age. Their power to flourish, making conscious choices, emanates from inside and is not granted by others, no matter what the family values or religion. We can live so much more joyfully when we know we do not have to seek permission to create our own lives.

> My mom ran my house when I grew up, but she always let Dad think he did. She just agreed to everything, then went ahead and did it her own way. Absolutely, she was my heroine.
>
> *Liza, veterinary assistant*

Had I written a much easier life script, I would not have had nearly the perspective I do now on presenting our wisdom traditions as we raise children. A structured spirituality, if that is what you choose, needs to nurture the open mind. Children need to *see* themselves in God and feel represented in myths and stories that lend insight on our human frailties, guiding us on the struggle for self-definition. There should be no fear or guilt when stepping outside established boundaries, as personal strength is developed by finding the truth of our own experiences. With this insight, when our girls are encouraged to grow beyond the constraints we experienced in our own families, they can avoid years of useless questioning of their own self-worth.

In my strict household where Dad ruled supreme, our father seemed congruent with Our Father. Dad was Zeus. There was no "Mother who art in heaven," so I felt Mom wasn't recognized. I remember wanting desperately to please my parents, while my brother and boys in general were so aptly glorified through the antics of football, other sports, and various male cultural achievements. I was taught never to disagree with my father, to be at the door waiting when he returned from the office to greet him, not to swear, to choose a logical career that fit well into the lives of others, and to learn the advantages of getting married. He refused to hear any complaints about my mother or have any discussion at all about her. I learned early on that emotional expression, in the form of tears or anger, was a sign of weakness. Housework was praised, as was staying home. I was often reminded that women were helpless, and I felt I was an inconvenience.

Sexuality was an off-limits topic in our house, so I was not even allowed to watch *Love American Style* on television because it was considered inappropriate for me, a teenager at the time. I was told sex was a duty to my husband. Menstruation was referred to as "the curse." There was no celebration of my body when I eased into bras, cosmetics, shaving, or anything a young woman considers a modern rite of passage into a woman-body. A class on human reproduction at the YMCA was the only insight I had into how men and women made love. When my parents explained the birds and the bees, they used non-descriptive language such as "women's private parts," so I didn't even understand how women got pregnant. The entire subject of birth control was off-limits; marriage was considered the prerequisite to sex, and even within marriage, birth control was not sanctioned. I felt blemished and contained, wondering why I ought to be denying the part of myself that included sex, boys, my body, being outspoken, exploring the world, and my desire to have a voice.

Organized religion was absent from my family life, as my parents chose not to attend church. Dad was a Lutheran and Mom a Catholic who was banished for years from her own family for marrying outside of her practice. There was little discussion about God, only the statement that we needed Him to live a good life. My brother and I were taught the Lord's Prayer, so God was clearly He. Although my parents had studied with a Bible group for years, I was never invited to participate. God was very, very silent in our house. He seemed to have a mysterious, private relationship with my parents that did not fully include me. My mother referred to God the Father and Lord Jesus often, but did not discuss scripture or even her own religion in any great detail, and Dad was silent on the matter.

As the years went on and I spent time at other people's homes, I realized that many aspects of my family's social structure were unhealthy and unbalanced, especially in relation to the role of women. There were countless unspoken messages on the subject, but by the time I finished high school, I was entirely confused. I began to sever all friendships and relationships, as a defiant way of proving I had power over my life. By the time I left home, I had difficulty generating the confidence I needed to feel successful in anything, all the way from school to relationships. I lacked focus and wandered intellectually for many years.

Despite the mystery shrouding God the He, the lack of structured religion did provide me with freedom to investigate my own ideas. As a child, I derived my own brand of spirituality from sitting outside in the woods, connected to nature, imagining myself in the center of a universal rotation. But it was cumbersome to put together all on my own, with no exposure to any alternative religions, philosophies, mysticism, or oral traditions of stories and myths that could anchor me in self-worth as a woman-girl. Not having any guidelines or encouragement to explore outside the male-referent system of my home life, I looked around for a religion and a God-champion that made sense.

There wasn't anything remotely accessible in religious symbols, except statues of the Virgin Mary, a positive female image because she transcended her carnal lust. There was no woman-Christ. So I read to find God, in countless books of science fiction, ancient religions, archeology, mysticism, and world religions. I discovered that a great deal of the Bible was crafted from men's stories and values, lacking a spiritual practice that nurtured the female point of view. I found extreme religions whose values are male-power-based, with social structures that dismiss women's human potential, considering women undeserving of education or medical attention and executing them for having sex outside of marriage. But I also found a wondrous aspect of God along with the Goddess, who affirms a woman's power and personifies a woman's natural processes as sacred. With the addition of She-God, I trusted my own power and the power of other women in families and society.

> I always loved being around things that smell good and look beautiful, so I work with flowers. Now, I am in spring and summer all year long. I say to myself, "I am these things. I am part of all this creativity." I become the flowers. I get to bloom every day. No kidding, this job is better than therapy.
>
> *Ellen, florist*

So I prayed to the planets, to the spirit in the woods behind our house, to the azure blue midwestern summer sky. As a child, I created my own holidays and rituals in my mind, searching for powerful She imagery for reinforcement; I found ships and tropical storms. But I learned to become comfortable with this. I found God in the birthing of kittens on our back porch, and in communicating with the wide assortment of wild birds and other stray animals we rescued off the street. I found Her in my dreams, in my psychic experiences, and later in my own children. God was also

Mother Goddess, who transformed life through divine compassion, my moon cycles, and my own acts of compassion that plowed my fields of frustration and self-doubt into self-love. God became a part of me because in order to cope with the demands of life, I needed to deeply embrace Her within, instead of accepting a God defined by everyone else.

As adults, we can reflect on those areas of life that challenge our self-worth, weeding out the residual self-doubt arising from old wounds. It *is* possible to reclaim yourself and adopt the "Divine I" as your self-image. No one is ever too damaged from their past to prevent recovery from such experiences. If we want to grow, becoming God comes from the realization that it is possible to redesign our self-image to one of splendor. And we have to rely upon ourselves, not others, to provide us with the image.

At the age of thirteen, I had a serious car accident that left me with a nose on par with a heavyweight boxer's. After initially healing from the crash, I visited a plastic surgeon with my father. The surgeon was to help determine whether another operation was warranted to correct the remaining damage. I remember sitting across the desk from the doctor as he reviewed my file. After a great deal of discussion, he looked at me, then at my father, and loudly proclaimed, "Face it. She's *never* going to be a great beauty." His prognosis was the determining factor on what to do with my face, my window to the world. I was stunned.

What I needed at that moment was for my dad to stand up and cite my fabulous qualities, walloping the doctor out the door. However, my dad seemed to have neither the words nor the astuteness to argue with him; he sat there and quietly accepted the doctor's pronouncement of my physical potential without resistance. And I was expected to accept it too, for the time being, because Dad's objections, if he had any, unmistakably went unvoiced. At that point, I realized my place: my world included authorities who had the power to reduce me to insignificant rubble. Having no financial or legal resources to change my circumstances, I could not challenge either man's opinion. I retreated into myself, too young to have a voice and ashamed to be a woman-girl. I felt unworthy.

We can travel on a healing path by replacing self-doubt with self-worth and staying in the present, not creating the present as a knee-jerk reaction to past memories. In my own experience, I could choose to live life feeling unworthy, but rather than bring unworthiness into my present circumstances and relive it, I chose to make peace with my past. Raising children and cultivating their sense of self-worth is a good exercise.

A few years ago, I discovered that my boys affectionately perceived me as the much-feared voice of reason when it comes to school policies or issues of community controversy. It's important that we not shy away from controversy and that we show our kids we will help champion their causes if it means enhancing their confidence and feelings of self-worth. They see they are worth the effort. Be their advocate, flex your muscles every now and then, as a tribute to those who cannot, no matter the place or time. As a measure of correction to my own past, I also talk with my boys about female achievement, God the Mother, women's history, female anatomy, and other female mysteries. We regularly converse (joyfully!) about the goodness of sex and self-image. They love it, and continue to grow up knowing that women are capable.

BUILD SELF-WORTH THROUGH A WOMAN-AFFIRMING SPIRITUALITY

In an effort to discover an organic spirituality, women are searching for a more authentic spiritual expression. They want to reclaim their original goodness and release cultural, personal, religious, and family messages that stress the truth of their existence and not their deficiencies. Sacred circles are springing up online as places to share insight, using discussion, ritual, journaling, and other creative methods to lend new meaning to self-development. A live circle is an invitation to heal old wounds and rejoice in the daily experience of being female, whether it's about conducting a sales meeting or diapering a baby.

Because these groups are interested in models of rotating leadership, they are uplifting to women who want to explore a sense of their own power. Groups encourage women to recognize the Divine within and shed the old status of womanhood. Women practice self-praise and affirmative thinking (the power of the mind to create reality) in order to exercise authority over their lives and revisit an earth-centered perspective, as in ancient times. Therefore, practices of these groups usually address seasons and cycles of nature in an effort to respect the female body and its natural rhythms.

Because culture has objectified women for so long and stressed age-defying mechanisms to prevent loss of a woman's power in the form of physical beauty, circles provide space for rituals that celebrate life's significant passages – menstruation, childbirth, menopause – and the wisdom of accumulated years. The body is honored. Women celebrate the Divine through movement and dance, performing songs or poetry, letting go of taboos that alienate women from their cycles and rhythms and instill a sense of sacredness about their bodies in every season of life.

> It would be great to learn more about the Goddess. If that would let me let loose for a day, great. I think I could really use that.
>
> *Pamela, police station desk clerk*

As a former creator of simulated environments for learning, I know well the value of experiential learning. I remember one circle when a young woman said she wanted to reclaim her body and celebrate her femaleness through movement. She stood up and, in an impromptu dance, spun and flew about with such joy and dedication to herself that it made everyone present dab their eyes. After we had put on some gospel music, it became contagious – we all felt like doing the same, because we so rarely remind ourselves of our incredible, beautiful selves. It felt great.

As a group participant over the years, I can attest to the therapeutic benefits of such simple and impromptu self-reclamations, especially when they address the damaging impacts of patriarchical language dictated by non-woman-affirming religious myths and theologies. Women *want and need* to formally recognize their own divine substance, especially through ritual. At another retreat, a woman confided to the group that she had never felt worthy because being female in her family meant she was "damaged goods." Her life was full of parental messages stressing that boys were a triumphant creation of what was right. Girls were a cursed reminder of the Eden myth.

We created a simple "womb circle" with about fifteen women in a surround, and pushed her out of the center. She imagined her own birth, thrusting from fresh and sacred quarters into the present – a new, unblemished life filled with purpose. We blessed her body by throwing flowers and petals on her and created a word montage, calling out positive messages from around the room about her innate strength and divine power to manifest her new world, including positive images of self. Does it seem silly? She later told me it was a liberating experience, allowing her to openly acknowledge her past and move forward. She was surprised by how powerful the ritual was in changing her belief system about herself.

Self-affirming rituals help women to be consciously aware of the present, reminding us we are all in the process of becoming our authentic selves while we welcome our humanness. Circles provide tremendous insight into a woman's values and behaviors. If women can develop deeper understanding about their motivations or life challenges through experiential means, then we ought to loosen up and uncork our Goddess within, in an effort to verbalize our past and create new memories that empower the present.

Circles stress community building, reminding participants of their connection and solidarity with all women, past, present, and future; but they celebrate life in the present. Women generally build self-worth by receiving validation for shared human experiences. They also are beginning to recognize the benefits of female ancestors, with some groups shoring up support for the feminine dimension of their own wisdom traditions in the form of the Goddess. Women are weary of the institutional propelling of old ideas that do not stress the authorship of their own lives. In the many groups I have led, a familiar theme crops up: women just feel good when they celebrate being an embodiment of a divine mother, a deity who represents the accessible, tangible dimension of life and gives them *permission* to feel empowered. Even though women haven't had much experience in the last few thousand years at including a female deity in spiritual practice, it seems the Goddess, in impromptu and unexpected ways, resonates with our desire to become greater than what we were told.

Perhaps humanity's challenge is not only to rebuild our self-worth where needed but, in the process, to reconcile our differences on what the Divine is. As a society, we are still so far from transcending gender in our image of the All that we must rely upon imagery that brings us closer to spirit, an abstract language that makes us believe we are all cut from the same cloth. We're so committed to our texts and mainstream interpretations, we've lost the ability to consider why we are born in the flesh: we are in charge of our own becoming. We need to create our own definition of spirituality, not rely upon someone else to make

> When I started loving myself, life became easier. Not just liking, but loving. Even appreciating my body. I didn't let family problems bother me any more. I made many new friends. I wish I had done it sooner.
>
> *Elise, tour guide*

sense of our individual journeys or argue over who is the correct messenger to deliver the message. Words are meant to enlighten us and help us resonate with spirit in our own unique way, not to outline strict rules of behavior or add more distance between us and our source.

As women, we have tremendous opportunity to heal old wounds by revealing our inner Goddess, or reclaiming our divinity. Through folklore, mythology, even scripture, the ideas already exist. Woman is not a subset of man, nor an insignificant part of God, but a powerful, incredibly beloved, and treasured part of a Mother/Father spirit that functions congruently in the evolution of our group soul as humanity.

Through many ancient writings, the principles of the divine duality of God and Goddess informed archetypes of every complementary pair that existed. She is the appearance of his essence, and the mirror of Him. The Mother represents the multiplicity of all forms, the coming into being, while the Father remains pure intellect. She's the soul, the physical manifestation evident in what we see in one another and on earth. She *is* Mother Earth. The Father represents order, the idea, or *being*, while Mother represents life in the flesh, the experience of living, or *becoming*. Father cannot identify with idea until He witnesses idea through the Mother. He is eternal and She is temporal. And in chorus, through us and the world we experience, they are continually being perfected by our participation in life. We are the creatress as much as we are the creator.

Without affirming the Divine within, we will never be able to feel worthy. Both inside and outside our circles, our self-images of success depend upon this simple recognition. We can't achieve the benefits of affirmation, neural networks, or our wisdom traditions without changing this fundamental assumption. It helps us live life consciously with powerful choices based upon the present.

CHRIST CONSCIOUSNESS AND THE SYMBOL
OF THE DIVINE FEMININE

Christ's universal story is an instruction on transcending the body, taking along the psyche/soul for the ride. It begins with an awakening to our own divinity. He represents the *journey* of consciousness, or evolution into our authentic self through desire and imagination, as we learn to identify with our source. Christ shows us what we are capable of when we choose to live in a state of conscious awareness, knowing we are an embodiment of spirit. His journey is about converting *becoming* into *being*; his trials parallel our own, encountered on the path to self-discovery through *gnosis*.

Gnosis refers to the *self-knowledge* we must seek during our life journey. In the Secret Book of James, one of the early Christian texts discovered at Nag Hammadi, Jesus speaks about living with faith, loving, and doing good works, all three ingredients of "demonstrating the Word" as a way to obtain self-knowledge. "This is how you can acquire the kingdom of heaven," he says. "If you do not acquire it through knowledge, you will not be able to find it." In other words, Christ consciousness is achieved through practice and effort, and an inquisitive attitude, when we peel away our physical self-image to reveal our true self on this plane of existence.

By adopting these simple and straightforward principles, Christ illustrated how to achieve oneness with spirit, living as an observer of his decisions, manifesting reality in the process. His message is encouraging: it's possible for us to do the same *here and now*. We can make "heaven on earth" by living like a Christ (being one with the Father or eternal spirit) within the temporal realm of the Mother (the individual soul or psyche).

If we assemble all three elements, we have a triune: Father is spirit, Mother is the soul/psyche, and a Christ figure is anyone who symbolizes the embodiment of spirit, or "living" spirit in the flesh. Christ represents the unification of both He and She principles through matter or the body. Plato often referred to this trinity as the one, the consciousness, and the psyche. If we deploy them concurrently, we achieve Christ consciousness, or conscious awareness. The Gnostics called the trinity Father (spirit/male/he), Sophia (matter/female/she), and Christ (light/son/lord), but after Christianity expunged the significance of the Mother, it became Father, Son, and Holy Spirit.

In the Christian Gnostic tradition, the Goddess frequently appears as the nature of wisdom or, in feminine guise, as Sophia the Mother. In the journey to gnosis, Sophia (Greek for "wisdom") is the counterpart to God. She is the creative force that summons the uncreated into creation, providing instruction on how to be living spirit within matter. While Christ is seen as an embodiment of the Father, Sophia represents the entire self-development *process*, incorporating individual body and soul into the mix. Sophia is a spark of the Father as reflected in us. We *are* Sophia as much as we are the Father or Christ, because our path to self-development includes our experiences, our emotions, and the earth as a living organism.

The goddess Sophia, as well as other numerous manifestations of Mother God that are evident throughout the world's religions, is hidden in allegorical references in scripture. Sophia is divine, denoting the feminine aspect of the totality of God, or the All, as immanent in creation. The Goddess is the temporal part of the plan, often seen in nature metaphors such as grove, dove, rose, lily, moon cycles, primordial womb, consuming fire, or life-giving waters. This universal earth mother, or the world soul, moves the creative process of the universe along, providing wisdom needed to navigate through our incarnational earth lessons.

If we live with awareness of being a Christ, each of us becomes a unique expression of spirit through the soul-body, where each undertaking grows to be an act of worship. As our authentic self is nurtured, life then takes on greater meaning as a present-moment experience. Through the power to manifest each thought, we can purposely create a world where we help the big mystery unfold. So, as long as we are consciously aware, everyone transcends as a consequence of having an individual soul and a body.

Sophia, the Mother of All Living

The ancients recognized that the process of self-development was impossible without the Mother, and they integrated the idea of feminine wisdom in their spiritual practices. Some glorified Her through ritual and religious poetry. Among the many mystics and teachers who wrote about the Mother was Philo, an Alexandrian Hellenist and Jewish Gnostic in the first century. His writings provided a philosophical bridge between the Greek written tradition and Christian Gnosticism, drawing upon Judaic and goddess lore for Mother Sophia imagery. Philo considered Sophia the divine counterpart to God in the creation of the universe, an active agent in the personification of God's goodness, and the "mother of *Logos*." Logos, the Word, was the guide leading to gnosis. He spoke of God's transcendental partner, associating the Mother with the goddess Isis, and created a literary composite of wisdom as feminine power.

In the Secret Book of John, Sophia is referred to as life, the Mother of the living. In this early gospel, Sophia represented a divine principle, giving birth to herself. The living tasted perfect knowledge *through* her, in an eternal realm conceived of thought. Here, God must be experienced through cycles of birth, death, and rebirth in many lifetimes, which are all avenues to achieve wisdom. Through Sophia the Mother, our gnosis is within our grasp.

Sophia survived in the first century B.C.E. in the Song of Songs and other wisdom books of the Bible, including Proverbs, Job, Wisdom of Solomon, and Ecclesiasticus (Sirach). Wisdom, Proverbs, and Sirach contain the major references to Sophia, where she appears as the feminine counterpart to a masculine deity, laying a foundation of values for the world. Her qualities are described as light, truth, compassion, justice, insight, and the hidden law ordering the universe, all qualities reflective of a divine presence.

> Mother God? It just might get my clients out of their body for a minute and quit worrying about every little roll of flab. They are so worried about getting older. You can't prevent aging – you still have to feel good about who you are.
>
> *Marlene, fitness instructor*

Solomon describes Sophia as the female personification of wisdom. In these passages, she is "the breath of the power of God, a pure emanation of the glory of the almighty, a reflection of eternal light, a spotless mirror of the working of God and an image of [God's] goodness" (Wisd. 7:25–27). Conceptually, she is a mirror of the Father, or that which provides the active, individual expression of consciousness within each and every one of us, through a body and soul. She demonstrates the essence of Him, as spirit expressed in the individual. Solomon was said to have a mystical relationship with Sophia, receiving divine knowledge from her, supposedly accomplishing divine works through her help and guidance (Wisd. 7:17–22, 8:2, 16, 18, 9:8–11). He speaks of wisdom being more precious than jewels, unsurpassable by anything one could desire. "Long life is in her right hand; in her left hand are riches and honor. Her ways are ways of pleasantness, and all her paths are peace," he says. "She is a tree of life to those who lay hold of her; those who hold her fast are called happy" (Prov. 3:13–18).

Sophia speaks about existing before the creation of the earth, as a co-creator being "brought up by him beside him like a master worker," "his daily delight." This passage speaks to a condition where all sons of men rejoice in the inhabited world and delight in the human race. It also refers to her as eternally one with the godhead, but also present in the world in the form of divine energy existing *within* the forms of creation. The natural world, as a repository of Sophia's creative energy, seems to be a place where the exchange between the Divine and the human begins. In other words, spiritual practice is realized through the joys of everyday living (Prov. 8:22–36).

Further dimensions of Sophia can also be explored in the Exegesis of the Soul, a Gnostic allegory that can be read as an account of a series of cosmological events pertaining to the creation, or individualization, of the human kingdom on earth in the form of the soul. The passage begins: "Wise men of old gave the soul a feminine name. Indeed she is female in her nature as well. She even has her womb. As long as she was alone with the father, she was a virgin in the form androgynous. But when she fell down into a body and came to this life, then she fell into the hands of many robbers."

The myth continues to make a parallel between the soul's journey and the feminine presence, who is depicted as a woman who is seduced (fallen), becomes a prostitute, but later remembers her authentic self. She asks the Father to restore her, and he "turns her womb from the external domain" so she can regain her true nature. By turning inward, she is purified and prepares herself for her brother-lover, her "bridegroom," and devotes herself to her identity with spirit. As the bride and bridegroom make love, they are united as one in a sacred, mystical marriage, a joining of body and soul (Sophia) and consciousness (king/Christ), symbolizing the complete realization of gnosis by everyone. After the marriage she returns to the Father, whole unto herself, once again a bride, or virgin.

A womb turning inward symbolizes the inner self purifying the ego, or a person who identifies solely with physical form. Enlightenment occurs where the voyage culminates: in the mystical marriage between Sophia the fallen, incarnating the human elements of the lower self such as earth and body, and Christ consciousness, our higher, immortal self, who is actually the Father reflected in his son.

The Goddess represents the journey of reconciliation of our essential natures. By becoming individuals born to face a lifetime of experiences, we lose knowledge of our true nature. Falling into ignorance, or becoming lost in the identification of appearances, is a familiar theme in countless creation myths. If our world of illusion is shattered (remember, we are spirit, not the body), and we find our way back to our source through self-knowledge, Sophia can transform us into "purified consciousness" or holy spirit if we choose. Together, Father, Sophia-Mother, and Christ represent the path to enlightenment or the return to our source of love through self-knowledge.

Overall, I think our spiritual evolution is better explained with a divine feminine presence. Jesus says in the Gospel of John, "No one comes to the Father but by me," which actually means that the *way* to the spiritual self is to know your essential nature. To transcend, you can't circumvent the Mother, because She makes it possible for your journey to happen! She is a beloved and amazing part of our self-development formula that cannot be bypassed. She is undeniably present in you as long as you are here. It is through her process of life and death, of body and soul, that we discover, learn, and are given the choice of how to *live* the idea of conscious awareness, or consciousness while in the body.

SHAKTI AS THE DIVINE FEMININE PRINCIPLE

In Hinduism, the female quality of spirit is represented by Shakti, whose name means "power." She is an aspect of the totality of spirit. In Indian culture, female spirit pervades the entire universe.

In Shakti's absolute state, she is pure spirit like the Father, but spirit *manifested* because she is the representative of the spiritual and natural sides of the universe. As matter, she is known as Maya-Shakti.

The male spiritual quality of the universe, or the male expression of the divine, is known as Shiva, who represents inert spirit giving Shakti the impulse to create. Both universal powers, Shakti (energy or power) and Shiva (static knowledge), constitute the spiritual background of the universe. Their dance is an exchange of the physical and the transcendental, matter and mind, one of emotion and intellect in an eternal embrace, or a sacred, mystical marriage. They represent a fundamental polarity where two are one, consciousness and bliss, in an absolute state of being.

Hindus believe Shakti is inherent in all things animate, as she is the animation of all living creatures. She is realized everywhere. In her absolute state, she is not bound by any physical limitations because she is a divine principle, a reflection of spirit, or matter demonstrated. One who practices the religion of Shaktism, a Shakta (Śakta), worships supreme deity exclusively as the female principle: as life is considered sacred, so is the power and capacity to make life manifest. In Shaktism the Goddess (the Mother) is the personification of primordial energy and the source of all cosmic evolution. She's the material cause of the universe to which everyone belongs.

> Mother is the deep dark of night, the moon. Father is light and sun. I like being moon. I've always loved the moon.
>
> *Christine, jewelry designer*

In this tradition, Shakti is considered the great universal mother because the feminine principle gives birth to spirit/consciousness, the male principle, in a manifested state; consequently, there is a deep communion with nature and the human body. The body is not objectified because it is considered part of the Great Mother's body. A Shakta has the potential to be consciously awakened to his or her spiritual nature by identifying with the Goddess.

Since Shakti is the force that makes all life possible, she is the feminine counterpart to personified male deities and represents their power or energy in the female form. There are various manifestations of the Shakti force, each with a god, a manifestation of the male god Shiva. For example, Sarasvati, the goddess of learning and wisdom, is the creator god Brahma's female half, a parallel to God and Sophia. Vishnu, the preserver, has Lakshmi, the goddess of wealth and prosperity. Parvati represents certain philosophical absolutes in her association with Shiva. She is seen as his embodied power, the creative force of the cosmos.

Since Shakti's domain is the natural world, she represents constructive forces of creation, or the life energy. She cannot create without Shiva, who is the underlying consciousnesses. They are inseparable. In many artistic representations of Shakti and Shiva, she stands black-skinned on white-skinned Shiva, who lies inert. He represents the colorless form of spirit, or transparent "light," since color is defined by the material world. She is the object, he is the subject. Like us, she is temporarily separated from the light of the spiritual world; as such, she is as deep and black as the night. Traces of Shakti are seen in the Black Madonna of the Catholic church.

In many wisdom traditions, darkness has always represented the deeper spiritual element, compared with the light of day. The union of light and dark constitutes the universe in its totality. The Sanskrit words *sat-chit-ananda* pertain to this totality, meaning "being-consciousness-bliss." Bliss is the result of unifying being and consciousness, Mother and Father. In Shaktism, living the highest spiritual truth allows life to be blissful, a union of Shakti and Shiva within oneself, with one's energies liberated through living.

In Hinduism, the motherhood of God, or the divine feminine, was expressed in many hymns, but none so beautiful as the Devi

Mahatmya, composed around 400 C.E. This describes the Great Mother's perfect mystical balance: she is understood to have both transcendent and immanent characteristics. The manifest world (matter or the natural world) and mind (our imagination, will, and thought) are Shakti's domain. Although she represents the material world, she is also composed of spirit in her purest state. In a passage of the Devi Upanishad that speaks of the divine feminine as encompassing both the known and the unknown universe, she is asked, "Great goddess, who art thou?" She replies: "I am essentially Brahman [the absolute]. From me has proceeded the world comprising Prakriti [material substance, active power] and Purusha [cosmic consciousness, quiescent], the void and the Plenum. I am all forms of bliss and non bliss ... I am the entire world ... Below and above around am I."

Again, we have God and Goddess as matter and spirit, the He and She of the universe, in a perfectly balanced spiritual equation. In the Hindu imagination, after matter and spirit expanded and contracted in the form of all creation, they reached a *bindu*, a point, drop, or circle at the end of time. The bindu is a place of origin where all matter and spirit eternally rest. At the dawn of a new day, new creation will begin again. This spiritual resting point is viewed as the womb of the Goddess, where creation, preservation, and destruction of the universe occurs.

The divine feminine is supremely transcendent but also fully present (immanent) in every single living thing. They coexist in each other. As long as we have not arrived at our bindu point, we are still *both* matter and spirit, a creation that arises from a union of Purusha with Prakriti. Our Purusha self enters into matter, then awakens the various energies in that matter. According to the Hindus, this leads to the formation of a false self, or ego, which is what the Gnostics taught we must transcend to identify with the true self.

Conceptually, the feminine principle rests within the oneness of the male principle; however, on a practical level, the female principle is most significant in the material world. If we are to view life and work as a balanced, spiritual practice, we must find room for both ideas in our lives. Both the feminine and the masculine are present in the idea of the Divine, but each is meaningless without recognizing the existence of the other.

Affirm the Mother Within and Feel Empowered

Through centuries of religious re-engineering and reinterpretation of the facts to serve interest groups, we've lost touch with our Mother and the sacred feminine principle. The association of the female with falling into an "ignorant state" like Sophia's (a temporary loss of spiritual identity) has brought many negative connotations for both men and women, but especially for the female gender. The concepts of original sin, being born in sin, or having a sinful nature because we are in a body have all been old, guilty leftovers from a time of suppression of women's religious rites and changes in political structures.

> The world would be so different with the Goddess. We'd have women coming out of the closet left and right, without makeup, speaking their minds. Women would finally quit worrying if they were smarter than men. They could just let themselves be.
>
> *Carol, women's workshop attendee*

Somewhere along the way, a set of values evolved that did not include what matters. We disregarded the natural world, as subservient or "bad," in contrast to a transcendent, "good" spiritual world. Our self-image was divided at the abstract level, and we chose between the concepts of spirit/light/he/high and physical/dark/she/low. Along the way to enlightenment, the female caused man to be separated from God, and transcendence became the primary spiritual objective. Embracing the reason for our physical manifestation, in its glorious wonder, is important for both men and women, but absolutely critical for many women whose self-esteem and self-image are still derived from cultural messages of what constitutes the value of females in society.

Even today, the sacred significance of the body, sexuality, and the physical earth has not been articulated, remaining absent from our world. We have denied the body and soul and opted to go directly to transcendence without grasping the notion that our everyday emotional and physical lessons occur on the path to self-development. Values such as "rising above" our bodily state as a way to transcend temptation and evil deny us an opportunity to grow. And without identifying with our transcendent qualities, we can have only the pleasures we experience in life, our pain and sorrow, our physical limitations and triumphs, with no greater meaning. It's time to consider *both* spiritual elements equally important in the search for self-knowledge.

If we incorporate Sophia, Shakti, or other images of the divine mother already present in many wisdom traditions as part of our spiritual heritage, we will have acknowledged our own evolution. Remember, our self-image and our belief in what we can do mirror the Divine we claim as our own. Our outer world is a reflection of what we think and what we value. Through affirming our female creation energy, we revitalize our own power as women and shed old programs of a valueless self-image. It's the first step in creating a new reality.

We must imagine our source as Mother and Father, a harmonious interdependence of the very best in us. But first, our job is to revitalize the Goddess within. When we recognize the unity of these most beloved elements within ourselves, our world will be in balance. As human beings, we will internalize our potential dimension of the cosmic whole and revisit our purpose, which is to authenticate ourselves by being reborn through the grace of Shakti, as we are reborn by Sophia as a Christ.

WHY WE NEED HER

Fortunately for both men and women, we're all gradually moving toward the center in the spirit-versus-soul debate. We are ripe for a goddess revival in order to stop diminishing our own self-worth. With the amount of resources available at our fingertips, it's fitting to revive the positive elements of a feminist gospel. If we could read at multiple levels to differentiate between recorded history, politics, myths, and religious dogma and resonate with our truth, we would stop rejecting our Mother's rich symbolism in favor of an exclusively male and monotheistic Father or God image. This imbalance alone severely undermines a robust understanding of our own spirituality. Additionally, for those of us who are female, it severely limits our importance, because no divine element is commonly recognized in being female.

What happens when we identify with Sophia, Shakti, or any of the other representations of Mother God? We begin to know the divine feminine within and love her as we love ourselves. We can appreciate the benefits of the self-development process, so beatific in its complexity as well as its simplicity. Mother God is the indivisible you.

> As I get older, for some reason, church becomes so much less important. I just think about living with all I know, and keep on learning. I think God will understand.
>
> *Pat, parking lot attendant*

According to the Gnostics, inner knowledge, or the knowledge that All is one, is the state of being that includes experience. The mind, science, and rationality are not the end-all – they are only half of the equation. Inner knowledge cannot be an intellectual exercise alone, nor a spectator sport. We must plunge into our emotions and go through the full range of what is offered here, for the sake of our learning experience. Where mind and matter meet, as in Shakti and Shiva, you will find that both are necessary elements for a unified universe, and for a whole and balanced you.

The concept of the Great Mother bridges the gap between our source and the inevitable path to enlightenment. She gives meaning to life in the flesh, to the cycle of the many lifetimes it takes to refine our soul. We need to break out of our former conceptual parameters and permit God and Goddess to stand in balance within us, both the idea of form and the builder of form, in order that we may create a life of our own choosing. We will create it through our own self-discovered gnosis, our path of knowledge, which by the way of wisdom becomes divine illumination. The greater path to self is through both.

Consciously Create Your Day

Affirm your power within. You can adopt new mental programs of power, purpose, and unity, and make room for loving both parts of yourself through mental discipline. I hope the following affirmations will be helpful in drawing out your power within.

SELF-LOVE: FEMALE QUALITIES
I love being female. I am all seasons, all cycles, all elements.
Each breath I take is prayer as I connect with Mother Earth,
the great primordial womb. I see the Goddess in me now and
view the past with love. I am lovable and worthy of love because
I already exist in a symbiotic state of love with Mother God.
As I occupy my body of earth-femaleness, I walk with Her in
loving harmony.

RECOGNIZING MY OWN DIVINITY
I am the light that has found expression in what is manifest
on earth. I am both transcendent and immanent. I am conscious-

ness that seeks an answer to the meaning of self. By being present on earth, I help solve the eternal mystery. I am divine energy because I belong to the eternal and universal self, which is God and Goddess. We are all the universe, and the universe is me, the Divine is in me, spirit is in me, and I am composed of spirit, in an infinite pattern of light, an all-knowing web of love. I open my heart to receiving grace from who I am, which is love and light, me everywhere. In all things my living, infinite spirit exists.

FEELING PART OF A TRIUNE

I am consciously aware of my existence. I exist within Mother God, Father God, and the Holy Spirit that is demonstrated on earth. I am capable of demonstrating Christ consciousness in my life. I am a spark of the Divine, and I exist in an eternal state with my divine parents; therefore, I am a demonstration of the triune. I am He, She, and the Christ. I become one with the All as I accept the Divine within me. I am empowered by knowing I am spirit.

For more affirmations, see my companion book, *The Women's Book of Empowerment: 323 Affirmations That Change Everyday Problems into Moments of Potential* (The Goddess Network Press, 2005). Available through any major online book retailer or at www.thegoddessnetwork.net.

Taking Spiritual Inventory:
Make Room for the Goddess!

Analyze

Look at your image of the Divine as ancient societies did. Is it possible to shed light once again on Mother God? Does She have a place in your heart? Can the Goddess share the field with other images of the Divine? Ask yourself:

* What is my greatest source of spiritual comfort and love? Does that image nurture me and resonate with who I am as a woman? Does my sense of spirit fill me with a sense of value? Does my image of the Divine showcase both my feminine and masculine strengths?

* Do I take comfort in my current religious structure? Does it allow me to celebrate who I am as female? Does it value the essence of who I am? Do I see my authentic self represented through positive images in my wisdom tradition's literature and scriptures? Does my religious structure value woman as much as man?

* Is it realistic to think there is only one path to the source? With worldwide religions and spiritual diversity, could this be an accurate reflection of the diversity and complexity of the Divine? Do I believe others outside your wisdom tradition are less worthy than me?

* Have I devoted any time in my life to reading the history of my religion? Have I read about world religions and expanded my perspective? Do political and cultural climates as well as the shift of power structures affect the way our religions have developed?

* Do I believe that men and women are equally divine and have the same power to channel spirit, either through religious ritual, administering sacrament, or holding positions within religious organizations? Does our world reflect an imbalance in the way we conceptualize our own divine natures or delineate a difference between the spiritual capabilities of men and women? If so, how?

* Do I feel sinful just because I am a woman? If so, why? Have I claimed ownership of myths in my life that reflect and support social structures because they are convenient?

* Is the concept of female deity impossible to embrace? What holds us back from doing so? If our culture were able to consider females as sacred manifestations of a female deity, how would it translate into our advertising, or into education? What changes would we see in our professions and politics, and in what we value as a society?

* Do I have a deeply seated negative self-image because of my female body? What is preventing me from celebrating my female aspect: my cycles, my ability to generate life, my experiences that are uniquely female?

* What religious images have an effect upon my personal life? On my parents? On our culture as a whole?

* Do I revere the earth because it sustains our life force? If ancient societies believed the Goddess was immanent within all nature, earth, and the universe, why does our society disconnect from those ideas?

* Do I feel out of balance because I do not deeply believe I am divine? If I know I am a divine spark of the creator/creatress, do I believe I am as powerful as a man? If I feel a lack of empowerment, is it because I do not know where my power originates?

Affirm

Allow self-love to enter your life. Give a voice to your female experiences and consider those sacred. Know that you carry the Divine in you. Affirm that self-love is the foundation for all love. Write an affirmation about your female power that will guide you from this point forward.

_____

_____

_____

_____

_____

_____

_____

_____

_____

_____

_____

Walk the Talk

Making room for the Goddess in your life is about celebrating your God (Goddess) self, embracing your emotions, and knowing that each action and thought you take to live in the present moment is sacred. As you begin, draw the following thoughts into your everyday experiences:

* a passionate love of self and others
* an ongoing desire to expand your knowledge and experience of spirit
* an inquisitive mindset, one that questions life, using knowledge and experience to develop wisdom
* a deep respect for natural laws
* an appreciation for your intuitive capabilities

* loving your body and its wondrous complexity
* attuning the self-love channel toward others, which is love of spirit. True self-empowerment comes from knowing what is within you.

Enhance your spiritual growth as you take action on these thoughts. List your actions here.

_____

_____

_____

_____

_____

_____

_____

_____

_____

_____

_____

_____

_____

_____

Share the Spirit

Share ideas on how we have developed special celebrations to recognize the Goddess in our lives. Do you have any favorite books, poetry, rituals, journal reflections, or pieces of music that enhance your connection to the Goddess? Discuss how you embrace the Goddess and how She generates more self-love, self-awareness, and self-worth in your life. Discuss with your group the ways our families, organizations, communities, and nations have divorced us from the concept of Mother God as immanent in nature.

WHAT DO WOMEN WANT?

Different wisdom traditions have pictured the Goddess in count-less ways. She exemplifies our emotional human qualities: com-passion, insight, fierceness, the desire for community, the pain both from bringing new life into being and from loss. She is Mother, Mater, matter. Poetically, she is the river, the flowers, fields of nature, and the earth's clothing. She is our journey within and without, the path to our very soul, and a power symbol of a wom-an's divine heritage.

Throughout history, we have personified the Divine in order to lessen the distance between God/Goddess and ourselves. Only then do we see divine qualities reflected in the mirror. Whether in Sophia, Shakti, or other representations of the divine mother such as Kuan Yin, Tara, Isis, or Kali, what we really recognize is the sacred feminine in ourselves, in the form of a promise. She is the vehicle through which we *achieve* a state of being. We *are* Her at the same time as we are spirit/consciousness.

Having a deep appreciation for women begins with compre-hending the significance of the feminine. In Hinduism, every woman is said to be a manifestation of Shakti's power, believed to be inherent in the form of mothers, daughters, wives, and sis-ters. Men always ask, "What do women want? How do I please my woman?" I'm going to finally solve this conundrum for everyone: men need to better understand where self-defeating messages originate in women, and become partners in helping women assume their power from within. And women need to return the favor by understanding men's fears and lack of confidence. Female *is* powerful. But rather than letting female fears continue into the next generation, we ought to facilitate shared power, solidly rooted in a fully developed sense of being. True power is a reflection of equally divine principles, of Father and Mother God, of intellect and emotion. Someday, male and female will see God's perfection reflected in each other. There is no telling what greatness society will accomplish with such an act of love.

So we've all got old programming to overcome, and lots of work to do.

After considering what women have openly shared with me, I know this for certain: right now, women *need* the Goddess to think positively and feel empowered. And men need to encourage this love affair if they want to understand women. Women want to feel the Goddess within, celebrate their emotions, dance their feelings. They desire a grounded spirituality based upon their own life experiences, with rituals that celebrate their unique human qualities and values. They want to express their womanness, which does *not* include play-acting men's perception of how women should be.

Women are weary of listening to burdensome creation myths that make them a subset of man and responsible for humanity's downfall. They are ready to break old rules, compete on their own terms, reviving a woman-culture anchored in the divine feminine. They need to believe they can achieve spiritual awareness through their own ideas. Like men, women are created in the image of the Divine and come as a whole package, ribs and all.

How do we make it happen? We need to stop reacting and assume ownership of our gifts, growing our capability to lead happier lives by simply cleaning house. Old mental programs that don't support us in this complex world must be replaced by new, empowering thoughts, especially about self-love and the Divine.

We need to become observers of our own lives. If the Goddess helps women move the energy of self-deprecation to liberation, then let's bring Her on. Better yet, let's start advocating a cultural goddess revival, one so big that it scoops up the men in our lives and restores their feminine side to them in the form of a balanced perspective on the way the world ought to be managed.

In all faces of the Goddess, I see wisdom for the soul journey, the development of self. Growing our soul happens when we face the deeper facets of our humanness: the passion, grief, resentments, prejudices, and preferences. We choose to deny our body and emotions in favor of the transcendent principle because we think we don't need them to evolve spiritually. In Western society, we haven't figured out how to balance these two principles. Nothing is more obvious than the missing Goddess, evident in our sour relationship to the earth, a disdain for the intuitive, violence against women, and other social and corporate injustices. To evolve, we first need to heal by honoring the process. And there can be no healing until we embrace the *whole* self, reconciling both intellect and emotion.

In our minds and hearts, we must be aware of our own polarity, one that is simultaneously differentiated and united, one that exemplifies these two qualities. Sukie Colgrave characterized this goal as achieving a third state of being that is about neither control nor freedom alone but control *and* freedom both. It is about completely surrendering to your own nature and to the world with enhancement rather than the loss of individuality, understanding, and freedom. You are responsible for your conscious development of both principles, but only through choice will you discover that power.

When we allow feminine wisdom to guide us toward the authentic self, the work is never without consequence. Terror, fear, desire, and pain reside in life's everyday lessons. But some feminine direction will most certainly lead us to conscious awareness, by way of perseverance and love. Inhaling the world in all its complexity does give us an opening to our own potential, despite our initial perceptions. It's an opportunity to create an empowered life. And the more deliberate our path and our choices, the sooner we will experience joy. Creating heaven on earth will become real for us as we embrace our own unrestricted genius in manifesting the lives we desire.

REFERENCES

Over the years, the following authors have helped me to improve my outlook in life and craft a strategy for positive living. Hence, they have contributed to the creation of this book.

About.com. "Women's Issues." Page under News & Issues. http://womensissues.about.com.

About-Face. Home page, www.about-face.org.

ACEPT W3 Group. 1995. "Holograms." Department of Physics and Astronomy, Arizona State University, Tempe, AZ. http://acept.la.asu.edu/PiN/rdg/lasers/hologram.shtml. Revised December 14, 1999.

Ammann, Kenny. 1990. "Individuation and the Biblical Concept of Wholeness." Lambert Dolphin's Library. www.ldolphin.org/individ.html. Revised July 26, 2004.

Anderson, C. Alan. 1997. "Panentheism vs. Pantheism." In C. Alan Anderson and Deborah G. Whitehouse, *New Thought: A Practical American Spirituality.* New York: Crossroad. Online at http://websyte.com/alan/pan.htm. Revised June 23, 1998.

Baring, Anne, and Jules Cashford. 1993. *The Myth of the Goddess: Evolution of an Image.* London: Penguin.

Black Elk, Nicholas (Hehaka Sapa). 1997. "Grandfathers." SpiritWalk. www.spiritwalk.org/blackelk.htm. Revised December 8, 2002.

Campbell, Joseph. 1991. *The Power of Myth*. New York: Anchor Books/Random House.

Carnes, Robin D., and Sally Craig. 1998. *Sacred Circles: A Guide to Creating Your Own Women's Spirituality Group*. New York: HarperSanFrancisco.

Chopra, Deepak. 1994. *The Seven Spiritual Laws of Success: A Practical Guide to the Fulfillment of Your Dreams*. San Rafael, CA: Amber-Allen Publishing; Novato, CA: New World Library.

Christ, Carol P., and Judith Plaskow, eds. 1992. *Womanspirit Rising: A Feminist Reader in Religion*. New York: HarperCollins.

Colgrave, Sukie. 1979. *Uniting Heaven & Earth: A Jungian and Taoist Exploration of the Masculine and Feminine in Human Consciousness*. Los Angeles: Jeremy P. Tarcher.

Conger, Jay A., and Associates. 1994. *Spirit at Work: Discovering the Spirituality in Leadership*. San Francisco: Jossey-Bass.

D'Aquili, Eugene G., and Andrew B. Newberg. 1999. *The Mystical Mind: Probing the Biology of Religious Experience*. Minneapolis: Fortress Press.

Dillon, John. 1977. *The Middle Platonists*. London: Duckworth.

Dispenza, Joe. Untitled archived webcast radio programs on Beyond the Ordinary dot Net–KRSE: June 12, 2003; October 21, 2003; February 12, 2004. www.beyondtheordinary.net/joedispenza.shtml.

Eisler, Riane. 1987. *The Chalice & The Blade*. New York: HarperCollins.

Fisher, Mel. Mel Fisher's Treasure Website. www.melfisher.com.

Fox, Emmet. 1949. *The Mental Equivalent: The Secret of Demonstration*. Unity Village, MO: Unity School of Christianity.

Freke, Timothy, and Peter Gandy. 1999. *The Jesus Mysteries*. New York: Three Rivers Press.

Freke, Timothy, and Peter Gandy. 2001. *Jesus and the Lost Goddess: The Secret Teachings of the Original Christians*. New York: Harmony.

Gadon, Elinor W., 1989. *The Once & Future Goddess: A Sweeping Visual Chronicle of the Sacred Female and Her Reemergence in the Cultural Mythology of Our Time*. New York: HarperCollins.

Gawain, Shakti. 1995. *Creative Visualization: Use the Power of Your Imagination to Create What You Want in Your Life.* Novato, CA: New World Library.

Godwin, Malcolm. 2000. *Who Are You? 101 Ways of Seeing Yourself.* New York: Penguin Arkana.

Hales, Dianne. 1999. *Just Like a Woman: How Gender Science Is Redefining What Makes Us Female.* New York: Bantam Books.

Harvey, Andrew. 1995. *The Return of the Mother.* New York: Jeremy P. Tarcher/Putnam.

Harvey, Andrew, and Anne Baring. 1996. *The Divine Feminine: Exploring the Feminine Face of God Around the World.* Berkeley, CA: Conari Press.

Hay, Louise L. 1987. *You Can Heal Your Life.* Carlsbad, CA: Hay House.

Hay, Louise L. 1997. *Empowering Women: Every Woman's Guide to Successful Living.* Carlsbad, CA: Hay House.

Helgesen, Sally. 1990. *The Female Advantage: Women's Ways of Leadership.* New York: Doubleday Currency.

Holographic Dimensions, Inc. "Holography FAQ." HyperMedia Technologies. http://hmt.com/holography/hdi/hdifaq.htm. Accessed April 2004.

The Holy Bible: New Revised Standard Version. 1997. Iowa Falls, IA: World Bible Publishers.

Institute of Noetic Sciences and Captured Light Industries. 2005. *What the Bleep Do We Know!? Study Guide and Manual for Navigating Rabbit Holes.* Online at www.whatthebleep.com/guide.

Kinsley, David R. 1986. *Hindu Goddesses: Vision of the Divine Feminine in the Hindu Religious Tradition.* Berkeley: University of California Press.

Koester, Hans. 1929. "The Indian Religion of the Goddess Shakti." *Journal of the Siam Society* 23 (July), Part 1.

LaTour, Michael S. 1996. "A Synthesis of Research for Managerial Application in the Pacific Rim." *B>Quest* (Richards College of Business, University of West Georgia, Carrollton, West Georgia). www.westga.edu/~bquest/1996/latour.html.

Learning Strategies Corporation. "Polyphasic Sleep." Discussion on Forum for PhotoReading, Paraliminals, Spring Forest Qigong, and Your Quest for Improvement. www.learningstrategies.com/forum/ubb/Forum4/HTML/000476.html.

Marcic, Dorothy. 1997. *Managing with the Wisdom of Love: Uncovering Virtue in People and Organizations*. San Francisco: Jossey-Bass.

Matthews, Caitlin. 2001. *Sophia: Goddess of Wisdom, Bride of God*. Wheaton, IL: Quest Books.

"Meister Eckhart." Internet Encyclopedia of Philosophy. www.utm.edu/research/iep/e/eckhart.htm. Revised 2001.

Meyer, Marvin W., trans. 1986. *The Secret Teachings of Jesus: Four Gnostic Gospels*. New York: Vintage Books.

Mitroff, Ian I., and Elizabeth A. Denton. 1999. *A Spiritual Audit of Corporate America: A Hard Look at Spirituality, Religion, and Values in the Workplace*. San Francisco: Jossey-Bass.

Morgan, Gareth. 1997. *Images of Organization*. Thousand Oaks, CA: Sage.

Newberg, Andrew. 2001. *Why God Won't Go Away: Brain Science & the Biology of Belief*. New York: Ballantine.

Ouzounian, Alice. "Who and What Is the Daemon?" Plotinus website. www.plotinus.com/the_daemon.htm. Revised February 2, 2005.

Pagels, Elaine. 1979. *The Gnostic Gospels*. New York: Vintage Books.

Pert, Candice B. 1997. *Molecules of Emotion: The Science Behind Mind-Body Medicine*. New York: Scribner.

Price, John Randolph. 1983. *The Manifestation Process: 10 Steps to the Fulfillment of Your Desires*. Austin, TX: Quartus Foundation for Spiritual Research.

Price, John Randolph. 1987. *The Abundance Book*. Boerne, TX: Quartus Foundation for Spiritual Research, Inc.

Richmond, Lewis. 1999. *Work as a Spiritual Practice: A Practical Buddhist Approach to Inner Growth and Satisfaction on the Job*. New York: Broadway Books.

Robinson, James M., ed. 1988. *The Exegesis on the Soul: The*

Expository Treatise on the Soul. The Nag Hammadi Library. New York: HarperSanFrancisco.

Roman, Sanaya. 1986. *Living with Joy: Keys to Personal Power & Spiritual Transformation.* Tiburon, CA: HJ Kramer.

Roman, Sanaya, and Duane Packer. 1988. *Creating Money: Keys to Abundance.* Tiburon, CA: HJ Kramer.

Rosener, Judy B. 1995. *America's Competitive Secret: Women Managers.* New York: Oxford University Press.

Rouse Ball, W.W. 1908. "René Descartes (1596–1650)," in *A Short Account of the History of Mathematics*, 4th ed. Online at www.maths.tcd.ie/pub/HistMath/People/Descartes/RouseBall/RB_Descartes.html.

"Ruysbroeck, Jan van." Encyclopaedia Britannica Premium Service. www.britannica.com/eb/article?tocId=9064528. Accessed February 21, 2005.

Satinover, Jeffrey. 2001. *The Quantum Brain: The Search for Freedom and the Next Generation of Man.* New York: John Wiley & Sons.

Shlain, Leonard. 1998. *The Alphabet Versus the Goddess: The Conflict Between Word and Image.* New York: Penguin Arkana.

Singh, Tara. 1992. *A Course in Miracles: A Gift for All Mankind.* 2nd edition. New York: Ballantine. (See also www.acim.org.)

Sophia Foundation of North America. "Who Is Sophia?" www.sophiafoundation.org.

Stace, Walter T. 1960. *The Teachings of the Mystics.* New York: New American Library.

Stone, Merlin. 1976. *When God Was a Woman.* New York: Harcourt Brace.

Talbot, Michael. "The Holographic Universe." Crystalinks. www.crystalinks.com/holographic.html.

"The Universe as a Hologram ... Does Objective Reality Exist ... Or Is the Universe a Phantasm?" 1991. Spiritual Endeavors. www.spiritual-endeavors.org/seth/hologram.htm.

Zukav, Gary. 1979. *The Dancing Wu Li Masters: An Overview of the New Physics.* New York: Quill/William Morrow.

Acknowledgments

While I was writing this book, my joy and gratitude have expanded because of:

My friends, who remind me that I am a beautiful, unique soul

My family, who believed in The Goddess Network from the beginning

All those in our worldwide electronic community at www.thegoddessnetwork.net, who share a part of their soul with me daily

My office staff and vendors, who provide positive energy in serving the greater ideas that bind us together

The book production team of Cattails; Peter Ross and Linda Gustafson at Counterpunch; my editor, Barbara Czarnecki; and my agent, Arnold Gosewich

My beloved doggies, who demonstrate the meaning of unconditional love each time I walk through the front door

And especially Mother God, who continues to provide infinite wisdom about loving my authentic self.

I thank you with all my heart for bringing more spirit into my workplace, my home, and every corner of my life.

About the Author

Charlene M. Proctor holds a Doctor of Philosophy degree from the University of Michigan and provides guidance through everyday complexity with female imagery and positive thinking. She is the founder of The Goddess Network, Inc., an organization for women who want to discover the feminine principle within. Her lectures, workshops, and electronic programs reach a worldwide audience daily. Although Charlene has written numerous papers on the subject of simulation, organizational learning, and recycling technologies, her material for a wider audience gives her the greatest pleasure. *Let Your Goddess Grow! 7 Spiritual Lessons on Female Power and Positive Thinking* and *The Women's Book of Empowerment: 323 Affirmations That Change Everyday Problems into Moments of Potential* are her two current works. She lives with her husband and two teenage boys in the Detroit metropolitan area.

About the Goddess Network Press

The Goddess Network Press publishes books on the Goddess, spirituality, personal growth, women's issues, simulation and learning environments, and positive thinking. We hope to make a difference in the lives of those who write books, as well as for our readers. Of course, we are in love with the Goddess and see our publishing company helping to spread divine feminine energy around the globe.

We believe everything on earth is a reflection of what is inside our heads. Our challenge in life is to allow our divine nature to work with ideas that make sense. A balanced world will be created by individuals who understand and embrace their true self.

As a member of the business community, The Goddess Network, Inc. is a venue for both live and electronic gatherings for anyone interested in expanding their intellectual and spiritual boundaries, especially women who want to nurture their spirit. We promote programs that foster deeper meaning and purpose in an individual's life.

Thanks for being our reader. We value your input and suggestions on this book and on others you would like to see published. Why not contact us? We are only an e-mail away.

The Goddess Network Press
233 Pierce Street
Birmingham, Michigan
48009 USA
toll free: 866-888-04633
tel: 248-642-1300
fax: 248-642-1700
e-mail: tgn@thegoddessnetwork.net
www.thegoddessnetwork.net

Visit Us at www.thegoddessnetwork.net

Inspire yourself and others through positive thinking by reading the affirmations posted on www.thegoddessnetwork.net under "The Women's Book of Empowerment." Mail them to your family and friends, even yourself, when you need encouragement. The Goddess Network is dedicated to helping women manage their multiple lives through greater self-awareness. Our job is to empower *you*. Join one of our electronic groups and send a positive thought to someone, or discuss the self-help exercises in one of our forums. Take us to Grandma's house electronically with your laptop and wireless card – there's no reason to be without inspiration and support! If you have a story to share, or an affirmation that will help other women get through their day, please register and leave your suggestion in our company mailbox at tgn@thegoddessnetwork.net. In this way, we can become something better together by supporting one another on our spiritual journeys.

The Goddess Network Online

* Send a free e-soul card!

* Register for *Divine Woman*, our free e-newsletter

* Join Forget Me Not™

* Participate in an online forum

* Visit our She Shop!

* Send an e-power thought

* View our movie *A Visit with the Divine Mother*

* Madame Pele's Bookclub

* Guest columnists

* See our Goddess Values

* Register for Charlene's live programs and lectures